F*CK
MONOGAMY:
Sexual Freedom is the New Normal.

SAHAR TAYLOR

F*CK Monogamy
Sexual Freedom is the New Normal
By Sahar Taylor

ISBN: #978-0-578-28635-8

Book design by jamericancreations.com
Back cover image by Arthur Brown
Printed in the United States of America.

First Edition 2022

Visit www.sahartaylor.com

To my Babycakes,

The happiness you seek comes from within.

Love you always.

Acknowledgements

I want to say thank you to the brave and amazing
humans who shared their stories with me.

I would not have been able to complete this
book without your invaluable input.

May you always live the life others only dream about.

CONTENTS

Acknowledgements vii

Preface xi

Intro 1

Monogamy Must Die 15

Sex vs Love 25

It's The Sex Energy For Me! 35

Lifestyle 101 45

The Lifestyle's Lack of Blackness 55

To Bi or Not to Bi 69

Non-monogamy In the Black 83

Agreements & Boundaries 115

How to Share Your Man 127

Insecurity & Jealousy: Your Worst Enemies 141

The Double Standard 155

Lifestyle Etiquette: Rules of Entanglements 165

Playmates & Playdates 179

Final Thoughts 199

References 207

PREFACE

Censorship in America is real. Freedom of speech and expression and your ability to exercise your first amendment right is limited by your willingness to only express yourself in a manner that is appealing to those in charge. The original version of this memoir, "Let Me Fuck Your Husband: Healing Black Relationships Through Consensual Non-monogamy," was, and still is, being censored. I was accused of "soliciting for sex," which was used as justification for the denial of advertisements on Instagram, Facebook, and other media outlets. The original cover, which displayed three Black, gorgeous, partially nude bodies in a sensual embrace, was banned repeatedly on anyone's site who dared to post the full-length version. *"It's because you used the word FUCK,"* they said. I challenge you to google *"books with FUCK in title,"* and you will find that several of them made it to the New York Times Best Sellers list and stayed there for years. So no, the use of the word FUCK wasn't the problem. Perhaps it was the partial nudity that put people on edge and made it appear as if it were porn. Maybe it was the audacity to make a statement such as "Let Me Fuck Your Husband" in an attempt to normalize non-monogamous sex, love, and relationships while also depicting three Black, gorgeous, and partially nude bodies. Without any other explanation besides "you have been denied due to the sexual nature" of the book, I was encouraged to change the title and the cover in order to keep the message alive. It wasn't an easy decision to make. It was my first book, and I spent a great deal of time, energy, and money getting it out to the public. I am very passionate about normalizing non-monogamy and non-monogamous culture. "Let Me Fuck Your Husband" was my first passion project, but I knew I couldn't be married to the title; I needed to be married to the message. The new title, "F*CK Monogamy: Sexual Freedom is the New Normal," seems to go down a little easier. Similar shock value, without the "solicitation of sex."

Monogamy, with all of its restrictions and conditions, is dying. It is a social and emotional construct created to control who we love and how we fuck. It's time for a change. How we view sex, love, and relationships must change. Although society at large isn't prepared for such a change, for the destruction of an ideology that is sewn into the very fiber of Western culture, the people are ready. More often, we hear about celebrity couples who participate in "open" relationships. I use quotations because "open" is just one particular type of non-monogamous relationship. When people don't know how to explain *those* individuals in relationships who share their partners, they label them "open," when in fact, they could be polyamorous, cuckolds, or swingers (More about this later in the book). Let's face it, most of us know someone, some couple or single person that refuses to be in traditional relationships. They may not say it openly to the world, but they exist all the same. Daily, I meet men and women who are bored with "mom & pop" relationships. They are more than eager to vocalize their discontent, as well as their overall lack of desire to be monogamous. The problem then becomes, "what kind of relationship can I have if monogamy isn't an option?" "How will anyone love me once I reveal I no longer wish to be in a relationship with just one person?" Once they expose themselves, the anxiety around the thought of rejection leaves many feeling lost and unsure if they'll ever find true love. That is where this book and I become useful. As a Lifestyle Relationship Coach, my goal is to guide individuals to exciting and pleasurable alternatives to traditional sex and relationships, with hopes they will find more gratifying ways to sustain love and stability through consensual non-monogamy or CNM. This book can be useful as a roadmap for you and your partner to properly navigate your journey through the non-monogamous lifestyle.

Oftentimes, we make relationship choices out of fear—fear of what we may lose if we don't make the right choice or the fear of not knowing where our choices will lead us. If you are afraid, trust me you are not alone. I used to be afraid as well. Like you, I never thought I could love someone and share that person at the same time. Like so many people, I believed that love was a sacred connection that two people shared. This is a common belief shared among monogamists. However, the notion that once you love someone, they belong to you and untouchable by others is an ideal that is fashioned from fantasy, selfishness, and insecurity. Only a minority of humans are capable of achieving the idealistic and heavily romanticized monogamous relationship for a lifetime. I had arrived at a point where I was willing to challenge what I believed about love and relationships because I didn't feel like I was a monogamist in my heart. Besides, everything else I tried leading up to that point hadn't worked.

Surprisingly enough, after twenty years of failed monogamous relationships, I decided to give non-monogamy a chance. This is how I discovered that loving someone meant allowing that person the freedom to exist as he/she was, which included the freedom to find sexual and emotional gratification in whichever way possible. "True love" can only exist in the absence of fear and possession. In other words, you cannot possess a person, claim he/she as untouchable property, then profess your undying love. That isn't love; that's possession. But we cannot possess other human beings. Humans are not property for us to own, and you cannot love wholeheartedly if you fear losing that person to others. When you make choices derived from fear, it's the fear that motivates you, not love, and fear is one hell of a motivator. I recognized that it wasn't for me to dictate how or from whom my partner received love or sexual fulfillment. I could only control how I loved, and I wanted to do so in absence of fear.

I embraced this ideal of love while participating in an open relationship and found value in sharing myself and my man with other people. I'm sure that sounds strange to you, loving while sharing. However, we openly admitted to each other what very few people are willing to reveal about themselves, that we needed to enjoy other people to be happy in any relationship. This wasn't because we didn't love each other enough; we loved each other a great deal. We just knew it would be impossible to have our needs totally fulfilled by the two of us alone and were willing to explore ways to ensure that both of us were happy. Now don't get it twisted; all of this was new to me. I didn't start at a place where I understood how to love, or knew exactly what our relationship would look like, or even how difficult it would be. To be honest, I was a fucking mess. It took time, a lot of emotional growth, stability, and maturity to get there.

This memoir is my journey to that place. Sharing this with you allows me the opportunity to help guide others who are fed up with doing things simply because "it's the way things are done." I decided to utilize my voice to help liberate other men and women who feel helpless in their relationships. So many people think about experiencing many of the situations I will reveal to you. The difference between me and the people who only think about it is that I actually do those things and love it; it is a lifestyle I've chosen. Within these pages, I've compiled some of my most intriguing and compelling experiences so that you may gain a more interesting perspective of non-monogamous culture. I would like for my story to be used as a road map, providing guidance on how to effectively initiate and participate in relationships that are quite different from the norm. I want you to use my experiences and those of other non-monogamists to guide you on your lifestyle journey.

My own journey was a whirlwind. Be prepared to read about my sexual entanglements as I shifted from traditional, monogamous relationships, including a marriage, quickly divorced, then journeyed into the world of non-monogamy in an open relationship. Once that relationship ended, I evolved into a Unicorn, having unique sexual and emotional entanglements with a variety of couples, discovering my true place among them. As I became heavily involved in the lifestyle, I recognized the lack of diversity in sexually uninhibited environments. That observation evoked my desire to open the hearts and minds of people of color everywhere to alternative forms of relationships. Please make note that the reference to "people of color" in this book is meant to be inclusive of any variation of Brown-skinned people from every culture. Occasionally, the reference to "Black folks" is made, speaking more to the culture of Blackness and less of actual skin color. Also, the reference to "couples" does not strictly pertain to those who are married or in legally committed relationships. At the minimum, it's two people who fuck each other.

Respect is given to the choices that every individual makes regarding sexual identity. This book does not seek to dismiss any gender or sexual orientation, but it is also not all-inclusive. This book was written specifically for people of color on their quest to achieve sexual freedom, be they straight, gay, or otherwise. This book is not about gender identity or equality. Therefore, in this text, you may not find who and what you identify as.

This book is also not intended to replace therapy. Still, it can be used as an informative text for those who struggle with the restrictions of monogamy and seek safe, pleasurable alternatives to achieve sexual freedom.

INTRO

"If monogamy is normal, why is infidelity so common?"

I fucked my first couple in 2017. I was on vacation in Negril, Jamaica, at Hedonism II, one of the few nudist adult playgrounds in the world. That year wasn't my first time there, but it was my first time while having the mindset of freedom and happiness over everything. By that time, I had been divorced for four years and was no longer willing to compromise who I was just to be in a monogamous relationship. I repeatedly hid myself from my partners, including my ex-husband, and I no longer wanted to live a lie. I had been married to a man who was jealous of his own shadow if it stood too close to me, so I was never comfortable talking to him about my desires for women or other men. However, once I was single, I was free to explore my sexuality in any way I chose. When I heard about the event at Hedonism or "Hedo" from a friend, it was a no-brainer. It was a chocolate-filled event, complete with nudity and public sex, and it was exactly where I needed to be. I had no idea that my experiences at Hedo would change how I interacted with both men and women forever.

"Welcome to the nude side!" some random, naked man said while standing on the balcony of his beachfront room. He then pointed to the big sign posted on a tree ahead of us, "Nude Only Beyond This Point (And we really mean it.)." We still had our swimsuits on but were quickly reminded of the "rules." Without hesitating, we disrobed, oiled up then ventured to the nude side. As the days went by, I realized that the sexiest and freakiest shit happened in the nude pool. And that is where I met the couple who really challenged what I thought I knew about myself sexually.

The wife was absolutely gorgeous! She had big hair, big breasts, and a body you would kill for. When we first saw each other, the attraction was instant. She was with her husband, who was also attractive, but it was she that got my attention. As I made my way to the swim-up bar, she approached me with a hug and pressed her beautiful breasts against mine. Our sex energy was crazy magnetic, and as we drank and laughed, all I could think about was what her pussy tasted like, and that thought alone made my head swirl. I immediately realized that a fire was set inside of me, and I refused to extinguish it, as I had so many times before. Prior to that day, I had been with other women, but none that had my pussy pulsating at the thought of burying my face between her thighs. I can't really say I considered myself Bi at that time. I just knew I liked women and was open to new experiences. As we chatted, I noticed the shade casting my way from some of the other women in the pool. I had just arrived at the party and had already won the attention of one of the hottest women there. Others wanted her, but she chose me.

We hit it off quickly in that atmosphere. Although I wasn't new to the environment, it was the first time I was surrounded by naked, sexy people partying freely, without the worry of being judged. If you haven't partied nude before, you're missing your blessings. There's something magical about nudity that changes how people interact with each other. The energy that exists in nude spaces is so powerful that you can't help but become deeply immersed in the atmosphere. When naked, you are truly exposed and forced to be more social and relatable because you can't hide behind the false façade that clothing creates. The nude environment is also highly erogenous and sexually stimulating, which will have you questioning and testing your boundaries in the most creative ways.

I never imagined I could desire a woman so intensely, but being next to her, feeling her bare skin brush against mine, smelling the conditioner in her hair as she swung it from side to side, aroused and amazed me at the same time. I watched her intently, how her lips parted when she smiled, the way her breasts bounced as she bobbed in the warm pool. The sun was blazing, which made the water glisten and reflect on her skin. I wanted her. My heart rate elevated every time she touched me. I had never been so drawn to a woman before. My sexual attraction toward her was powerful, and although nothing was verbally stated, I knew her husband was definitely trying to fuck. He watched us eagerly as we flirted with one another, but he played the back a bit, laughing, conversing, and getting us more drinks. He wasn't overly aggressive or annoying like men can be in those situations. He just chilled and let her work her magic. Although she was coming on to me strong, I could tell she wanted me to like him too because she kept saying, "Babe, she's gorgeous right?" as if not only to get his approval but to let him know I was who she wanted for them. He would agree with a nod and a smile. They would lock eyes and exchange unspoken messages. They were in tune with one another; this was what they both wanted. I knew some shit was about to go down that was unlike anything I had ever experienced, and I was there for it all.

I had never had sex with a couple before. In the past, I had been prop-ositioned a few times by couples, but usually from people I would never fuck individually. I had yet to be approached by two fine human specimens eager to tear my clothes off and have their way with me. From my perspective, I don't benefit at all if I have sex with people I'm not attracted to. What's the point in that? This, however, was the first time I had a sexual attraction to both partners. As we talked, I could feel the desire to have them burning deep inside me. If hot and bothered was a person, my face would've been front and center. Although I was already open to the idea of having sex with multiple people, she was the one that made me see how comfortable you can make a woman feel with fucking someone else's husband. She was constantly pushing us together and asking if he approved of me. She was also trying to ensure that he and I vibed as well. She knew what he liked, but she needed to make sure I was also on board to fuck him. He was cool. We shared some laughs and more drinks while she continued to work her magic. Her energy was infectious. It was almost as if she wanted me for him, more than for herself. That honestly was the part that really blew my mind. She was invested in his happiness. She knew what he needed, somehow managed to make that what she wanted, and then participated in actualizing his fantasies with him. It seemed so natural to me that I didn't think any of it was wrong. I thought it was perfect, really. They both get their needs met when they share each other in those experiences, which ultimately makes their relationship stronger.

The vibe we had was amazing, which eventually translated into great sexual experiences with them later. When we finally fucked, it was a movie. She tasted amazingly sweet like a fresh water hole in the Caribbean, and his dick was adequately sized to my liking. I devoured her pussy, licking all of the pink flesh I could find, trying to swallow any juice that oozed from her. I had never enjoyed burying my face into a pussy until I had hers. She was willing and wanting as she moved her waist to the rhythm of my tongue. She was also a great cheerleader for her man while he tried to fuck the life out of me. I, in turn, let them have all of me, tasting and touching me wherever they desired. However, she did need a bit of instructing from him when he wanted to watch her please me. He wanted to see his wife suck my pussy, while he hovered above my head with his stiff dick inside my mouth. Although I could tell she didn't have much experience in licking pussy, my intense desire for her and the experience with fucking them as a couple was enough to carry me through. He and I orgasmed together. My face was buried in her pussy while he deep stroked me from behind. He tried to save it for his wife, but she encouraged him to finish. "Get all that pussy, Baby," she told him repeatedly until he let loose. When he was done, I pulled her to me and continued to lick her wet flesh. He slid his dick into her mouth until he was firm again. Once he was able to slide inside her, she climaxed in a matter of minutes. After each of us came, we kissed and cuddled until we passed out.

That's when I realized how amazing fucking a couple could be. I know it sounds like it could be a messy situation, but something about the wife granting me permission to suck and fuck her husband while she kissed me and touched me was intoxicating. In those moments, I realized that this was more than just a threesome to them. This was how they bonded, how they stayed connected and kept their relationship intact. I wanted more of them, and I wanted what they had.

My Lifestyle journey had just begun, and it was off to a great start. By week's end, I had sex with another couple and orchestrated and participated in two different orgies. My mind was blown with the ease in which sex could be procured in that environment. After that week on vacation, I knew one thing for sure and two things for certain. One, my desire for women was going to enhance my sex life tremendously, and two, I would never be in a monogamous relationship or anything that looked like one ever again.

Fuck monogamy! I will never waste my time pretending as if one man had the capability of pleasing me. This is something that many of us do, men and women alike; play-acting as if we're so pleased with our partner; meanwhile, we're finding pleasure elsewhere. It is now 2022, and I am happy to see that more and more people are finding it within themselves to admit that monogamy is not for them. You would be surprised to learn the number of your friends, family, neighbors, and coworkers who actually practice some level of non-monogamous behavior within their relationships.

Is non-monogamy becoming the "new normal?" That seems to be one of the most jarring questions of the new year. During COVID 2020 and 2021, people were forced to stay at home in the company of their partners due to spiking COVID cases and deaths. If you were pretending that monogamy was for you prior to the lockdown, your relationship most likely took a turn for the worst. As if monogamy wasn't restricting enough, COVID stopped folks from interacting, touching, and fucking anyone besides their partner out of fear of catching the virus and spreading it to other household members. That said, when "Let Me Fuck Your Husband" dropped on Amazon in December 2021, book sales allowed me to see that folks were eager to find ways to introduce the "we should fuck other people" conversation to their partners. Hopefully, the book made it easier for many to not only have the discussions but to also decide if non-monogamy could work for them.

I was in my mid-thirties when I decided monogamy was not for me. Before then, I was like most other women, waiting for "the one" to sweep me off my feet. I looked for someone I could call my own, that would want me and only me. I had been in and out of relationships, falling in love then out of love, never once considering sharing my lovers as an option. So, I can understand why sharing a partner with others may seem inconceivable to you. I doubt that when I was married, I would have jumped at the chance to permissibly allow another woman to fuck my husband. Although when a relationship is rooted in insecurity, jealousy, and anxiety, as was my marriage, it was best that no one else was invited to that shit show. I'm sure when you thought you found "your person" and entered into your monogamous relationship, partner sharing was most likely not one of the agreements the two of you made. I know for a fact, it wasn't one of mine. Finding "true love" or "the one" is so deeply ingrained within us it's almost impossible to let go of the notion of having a "normal" union. But what happens when the "normal" relationship no longer works? What happens when the sexual desire for one another is muted, but the longing for sex and immense passion from others is much more intense? Those feelings and emotions will eventually surface during your relationship and could have a devastating impact if you aren't prepared to deal with what happens next.

Each of us knows what happens next. In a monogamous union, once you've proclaimed your love for another, you are not permitted to fuck other people or have an emotional connection with anyone else. Monogamy forces you to repress your sexual appetite and ignore your deepest desires, which many people find difficult to achieve. So what happens next? The side chick, the side dude, lying, deceit, disloyalty, more lies to cover up the previous lies, children born outside of the relationship, STDs, mental anguish, anger, fear, pain, violence, and unfortunately, sometimes death. And for what? Trying to keep up with a culture that was created to tame you and control you. Monogamous culture is suppressive and does not provide you with the mentality, emotional aptitude, or the tools you'll need to work through challenges pertaining to the lack of sexual and emotional fulfillment. If you're sexually unsatisfied in your relationship, you're supposed to grin and bear it. But what kind of fucking life is that?

Have you ever considered what you're supposed to do when you're bored with fucking your partner? Imagine that your sexual connection has withered and turned sex into an occasional activity you feel obligated to perform. I know what that feels like, fucking because today is Tuesday, and the last time was four days ago. That was me during my marriage, my last and final monogamous relationship. We were already in therapy and tried different things to spice things up, but I was bored out of my fucking mind fucking him day in and day out. Truth be told, he was probably bored of fucking me too. Most men don't want to have sex with the same woman all of the time. After they fuck a few times, every pussy loses its luster. I don't care who you are or how good your pussy is; after a while, it's the same "old pussy." Dick gets old, too, although most men don't care to believe it. So, the question is, what tools do you have in the world of monogamy to help you get over the innate desire to fuck other people? Some say have faith, trust in God, pray on it, or try therapy. Try if you may, but neither of those methods really work because monogamy goes against our most innate human instincts.

Monogamous humans are obsessed with finding a partner that they can have all to themselves. I can't count the number of times a man has said to me, *"I deserve to have someone no one else can touch!"* That isn't about love; that's about sex and possession of the pussy. While different forms of monogamy exist, most people only seem to be concerned with sexual monogamy, which is quite ironic considering it's the most difficult arrangement to uphold. Sexual monogamy specifically limits sexual contact to the two people in the relationship, with no outside partners allowed. Rooted in religious dogma, monogamy is so fundamentally flawed and unrealistic that not even the "godliest" of men can achieve the prescribed relationship of "one man and one woman" forever. Many well-known civil rights leaders, pastors, musicians, and athletes have been accused of, or admitted to, sexual misconduct and infidelity, not because they are bad men, but because they are human with the same desires as the rest of us.

Take your relationship into account. At any point have you or your partner been guilty of infidelity? If you can answer yes, it's understandable because studies have shown that more than 70% of individuals cheat at some point during their relationships.[1] Infidelity is one of the leading problems that ends most relationships, including marriages. If monogamy is normal, why is infidelity so common? I truly believe that infidelity has more to do with the problematic mores of monogamy rather than an individual's inability to be faithful. As a couple, you may genuinely love one another, but when that sexual fire is lit and your partner can't extinguish it, you will find someone who can. This behavior is not accidental, and those who transgress are not intentionally seeking to hurt their partner; they're just subjected to their humanistic need to satisfy their sexual desires. There is nothing natural about monogamy. Those who understand this logic have turned to non-monogamy as a viable and extremely satisfying solution to minimizing infidelity and achieving emotional and sexual freedom that doesn't exist in monogamous relationships.

Non-monogamy is the umbrella term under which many forms of relationships exist. From polygamy to open relationships, many couples from various backgrounds have chosen to form bonds that permit sexual contact and emotional connections with others outside of the primary relationship. You may not believe these types of relationships can work for you; however, your aversion to them is partly due to how you were nurtured into believing so deeply in the monogamous union. Non-monogamy may not be a highly favorable relationship style in this society; that's a fact. However, through partner sharing, you can find emotional and sexual fulfillment from others besides your partner and work on re-building the intimacy in your relationship while pursuing your own sexual freedom.

Sexual freedom is at the core of non-monogamy and non-monogamous relationships and flows from the belief that human sexuality cannot and should not be controlled. It is the most liberating mindset to have when seeking unadulterated sexual expression. When you are sexually free, you are unashamed of your desires, and you try to find ways to fulfill them, however unconventional that may be. This book seeks to help you realize the endless possibilities that exist when you embrace sexual freedom and practice a non-monogamous Lifestyle. This unconventional, yet appropriately timed text, aims to accomplish three things:

1. To help you un-learn what you've been taught to believe about love, sex, and relationships. The mind-fucking about sex and sexuality that was forced upon you your entire life must be undone. This can only be accomplished if you are ready to receive it.

2. To introduce you to a lifestyle that so many couples have turned to, to salvage their relationships. This book seeks to broaden your understanding of what it means to be non-monogamous, with hopes that it will rejuvenate your most intimate connections to your partner.

3. To help you become more sexually aware and achieve sexual freedom. Once you see the value in this way of life, you will be empowered to be your most true sexual self and seek ways to have your most intimate desires fulfilled.

Each of these can be achieved if you leave your judgments and preconceived notions behind and are able to read with an open mind. This book is not your typical relationship guidebook, and it is not for the faint of heart. It is fun, wild, provocative, and educational. However, it's also an eye-opener for those who have tunnel vision regarding relationships. I will share my journey with you and allow you to peek into some of the most intimate moments of my life to give you a realistic view of what it means to be sexually free and non-monogamous. Over twenty non-monogamous couples were interviewed for this book to give you a broader range of ideas that may be different from my own. Some of their experiences have also been included for realism and clarity. Names have been changed, and geographical locations excluded to protect the anonymity of my friends, lovers, and fellow non-monogamists. So, if you're ready to be amazed, amused, and thoroughly entertained, then let the journey begin.

Monogamy Must Die

"Most men cheat because they aren't allowed to express their true sexual desires to the woman they love."

My ex-husband was a cheater. He most likely still is. He cheated on his first wife multiple times, and he cheated on me before and after we were married. Actually, I was one of the women he cheated on his first wife with, so I guess I got what I deserved. His current wife is just one of the women he fucked while we were married. She knows what kind of man he is, but she waited on and fucked him through two marriages and married him anyway. Like most men, his desire for new pussy was something he hid from the women he was in relationships. With the exception of his close friends and the other women he was fucking, he kept his desires to himself *and got new pussy when he found opportunities to do so. I can't say that I blame him for cheating, though. The sex between us was good at first, but eventually, I was bored of it, so I know he was bored too. He wasn't very spontaneous, and no matter how many tricks I tried or toys and books on "how to have a better sex life" I bought, the sex was fucking boring. And because we fought all of the time, my desire to fuck him had dwindled so much that by the end of our marriage, I needed weed and wine just to let him touch me. I'm sure he could feel how distant I became. I refused to initiate sex anymore. I wasn't interested. So if he didn't come get it, he wasn't getting it. I would look at the calendar and realize it was Tuesday and let him fuck me just because it had been a week since the last time. He didn't seem to mind much, but, it all made sense once I realized he was fucking around.*

Have you ever wondered why men have such a hard time being faithful? Most think that men are weak and too immature to maintain a relationship with one woman. I believed that to be true at one point in my life until I decided to truly understand the nature of man and the institutions in which we are forced to partake in. Monogamy is one of those institutions forced upon us by society that makes life much more complicated than it has to be. The emotional and social construct of monogamy is so problematic that most who attempt it fail at least a few times, making sense, considering how we are conditioned from childhood.

From the start, men aren't nurtured to be monogamous; only women are. Men are free to fuck around with whomever they please, at least until their wedding day. He's just *"sowing his wild oats,"* they say, but even after the "I dos" are exchanged, getting caught with another woman is still a forgivable offense. On the other hand, a woman has been conditioned to believe that her vagina is her most valuable possession and to give it up too early or too frequently devalues her. They say, *"You must fall in love with the man you give yourself to. You must wait until your knight in shining armor sweeps you off your feet and pronounces his undying love for you. Then, and only then, should you spread your legs and give up your treasure."* I was told some semblance of this lie when I was a little girl. *"Be modest,"* my father would say. *"A girl that hangs around too many boys will look loose."* He once told my sisters and me that if he had a chastity belt, he would lock up our vaginas until we were married. *"A girl that gives her coochie away will never see her wedding day,"* he would say.

Sayings like these are told purely to control what a female does with her body, and from those sayings, a little girl grows up to be a woman who genuinely believes that her vagina is her most prized possession and that her husband will love her more for saving it for him. Although it is true most men value virginity, particularly in women they choose to marry, a woman's virginity or having minimal sex partners does not stop them from finding fulfillment in other women when they see fit. There is very little value, if any, in a virgin man. If a boy remains a virgin when he reaches manhood, he becomes the brunt of tasteless jokes that are difficult to live down. No father tells his son to save himself for his wife, at least not in Western society.

In most societies there is a push for boys to lose their virginity as soon as possible because getting laid brings a boy closer to manhood. Unlike young girls, little boys are not nurtured to save themselves until they find true love. Monogamy is purely a decision some of them make, but it isn't necessary. When they are misled to believe that they will someday find sexual fulfillment in the one partner they happen to fall in love with, they quickly realize they've been bamboozled into believing in the fallacy of monogamy, and it's not at all as gratifying as they were led to believe.

Studies have shown that 78% of men choose to cheat as a rational response to the irrational expectations of monogamy.[2] Once they start feeling entrapped by the restrictions and the inability to find fulfillment in the chosen partner, they step outside of the relationship to get it. Women don't like, nor do they appreciate, this behavior, but the truth of the matter is that the behavior is more aligned with the sexual nature of humans than monogamy is.

A quick lesson:

Humans are not biologically or genetically monogamous. Humans are mammals. Less than 10% of mammal species are monogamous. Lifetime sexual monogamy is exceedingly rare in the human species. Monogamy does not come naturally to humans. It is not the norm unless a society enforces it.

Don't you think it's odd that it's acceptable for you to desire more than one of almost anything else in life; more than one child, more than one car, more than one handbag, shoe, vacation spot, but never more than one love? The notion that once you find your soulmate, you suddenly lose interest in other people isn't natural, nor is it practical. Magically or by faith, you're supposed to shut yourself off completely, sexually and emotionally, from the rest of the world and only find interest in one person. One. Who created such foolishness? The harsh reality is that men fantasize about fucking different types of women all day, every day, and have little desire to have sex with just their partners.

Contrary to popular belief, many women share the same sentiment. Although a woman is more commonly content with one partner if she's satisfied in the relationship, they also fantasize about having sex or spending time with other people besides their partner. More than 50% of the women interviewed for this book stated that they couldn't be forthcoming with wanting other dick because their man wouldn't be able to handle it. For them, revealing the truth of their desires is not worth the backlash surely to be dished out by jealous or insecure partners. As a result, women also cheat to find whatever it is that is missing from their relationships.

It's no secret that most relationships experience some level of infidelity. But here's the thing, people don't cheat because they're dishonest at heart. People cheat because being honest about who they are sexually isn't acceptable in today's society. Men are notoriously known for having one or more side chicks. Yet, they continue to try to make monogamy work. The majority of the men I interviewed admitted to cheating in the past. Still, they did so because they couldn't be honest about their desires for other women while in those monogamous relationships. Unfortunately, many women can't grasp the concept of "sex is just sex" because the assumption is that love is minimized when you have sex with others. *"How can you love me and fuck someone else?"* is a common sentiment plaguing so many relationships and keeps people stuck in situations where sexual fulfillment is harder to achieve.

Ladies, I want you to be honest with yourself for a moment. Wouldn't you rather be in a loving relationship where your needs are being fulfilled, and you no longer have to worry if he's cheating on you? How many of your relationships have gone to hell because he cheated? I realize you desire to be his one and only, but you're fooling yourself if you truly believe that your pussy is so bomb that your man wouldn't want some bomb ass pussy from someone else. Yes, I said it. What's the old adage? *"Ain't no pussy, like good pussy, except new pussy."* That fact still remains true today. To be clear, CNM relationships will not stop a person who wants to cheat. A person who wants to cheat is going to be deceitful and conniving no matter what allowances they have within the relationship. What CNM relationships do achieve, however, is allowing partners the space to share true feelings, desires, and fantasies with the goal of creating more gratifying relationships that could eliminate the need to cheat. It's time to let go of the expectations from relationships of old and step into a more realistic understanding of what a loving relationship can be. For far too long, we've allowed society to dictate how and with whom we should love and have sex with. Once you relinquish outdated societal norms, it will be easier for you to unburden your mind and see non-monogamy as a method to having healthier, more fulfilling relationships.

How many of you have ever sat down with your partner and had a conversation about your fantasies? Do you have any idea what *really* turns your partner on? What if you found out that your partner secretly fantasized about sharing you with other people or desired to participate in group sex sessions? If the two of you could openly and honestly talk about your true sexual desires without judgment or shame, both of you may be surprised to realize you share similar fantasies. But these conversations won't happen if you let your relationship fall victim to society's shame game. Couples who practice non-monogamy have dropped the proverbial "normal" relationship in search of something deeper and more fulfilling. Believe it or not, millions of singles, partners, husbands, and wives are unapologetically non-monogamous, choosing to shape their relationships into ones that break the rules of traditional sexual and emotional bonds. Recent studies have shown that almost five percent of relationships are consensually non-monogamous. While not a very large percentage of people, the reporting of such relationships seems to be a growing trend. These individuals, and those like them, have chosen to tailor their relationships specifically to meet the needs of their partnership, not to someone else's ideal of what a relationship should be. We refer to this way of being as the Lifestyle. The Lifestyle, commonly referred to as LS, is living free of monogamy and monogamous views pertaining to sex and love. The Lifestyle is fun and exciting, and within it exists a world full of individuals seeking happiness in unconventional ways. I won't pretend like CNM relationships are perfect. But what I can tell you is that once you free yourself from caring how the world sees you and focus on how your partner loves you, you can begin exploring the Lifestyle together and ultimately find ways to have more gratifying relationships. Once you make the choice to free yourself and seek happiness on your terms, you will begin to understand what it means to be non-monogamous and truly immerse yourself in the Lifestyle. Exposing yourself and your relationship to sexy singles and couples could be the game-changer to the monotony in your sexual and emotional life as you discover what really makes you happy.

The first step to achieving this goal is understanding how you view sex and its relationship to love. This is where many women struggle with the idea of being in non-monogamous relationships. The "sex is love" myth is one that many women often believe and is at the heart of the unhappiness that follows them throughout their relationships. Most men do not give credence to the myth. Therefore, they remain true to their sexual instincts and act upon them with little consideration of lost love. This conflicting perspective is the most crucial notion of understanding and the most difficult thing for women to set free.

SEX VS LOVE

"The only relationship that exists between sex and love is the one you create in your mind."

Sex is not love. Sex is sex. I know there are a million books out there that try to explain what sex is. They describe sex as some spiritual and sacred experience two lovers share. I've read books about sex transmutation, where one uses sex energy to channel energy of a higher order, land a job, or build a home instead of using sex energy for actual fucking. Huh? What in the no orgasm ass shit is that?! What is sex energy for, if not to have sex? I'm so tired of hearing, *"Everyone you have sex with, you're having sex with everyone they had sex with."* This so-called logic is about control. Control over who, what, when, where, and how you have sex. How about this? I don't give a fuck. Sex is fun, and I do it for enjoyment. We all do it because we enjoy it. Whether you're young or old, rich or poor, married or single, you fuck because it feels good. Sex isn't spiritual, although I may have called upon God once or twice while getting my back blown out. But I seriously doubt my screams of a higher power's name have brought me any closer to spiritual enlightenment.

Love is not sex. Love is love. Love is unconditional; sex is not. When I love or fall in love, I fall in love with the person. For his character. For his tolerance. For his patience. For his honesty. For the joy he brings me and others around him. For the way he weakens me with his smile or warms me with his touch. For the belly laughs that make me cry and the nonstop jokes about asinine things. For his ability to share his true self with me. For his unwavering support of me and loyalty to me. Not how deep he digs my back out or how often he makes me cum. Love is much more complex than sex could ever be.

Sex and love aren't mutually exclusive. The two can be intertwined, but they are not the same. I know it sounds strange, but that's only because you've been taught to think one way, that love and sex go hand in hand. But the intimacy and sexual gratification we seek can be achieved when the parties involved agree that intimacy does not have to equate to love. I'm sure you've had amazing, mind-blowing sex, and considered for a brief moment that you could be in love. But, what if I told you that the hormone released in your brain when you have an orgasm is the same hormone responsible for the feelings that arise when you're connecting with your friends, bonding with your children, and falling in love?

Oxytocin, sometimes referred to as one of the "happy hormones," is a naturally occurring hormone in your brain whose production is stimulated during non-sexual bonding with parents, children, and friends. In women, oxytocin levels increase substantially during childbirth, causing the uterus to contract and aiding in breastfeeding when the nipples are stimulated. In men, oxytocin is produced in similar quantities as women. However, little is known about how it affects a man's body.[3] On a social level, oxytocin has a shared effect in both men and women, particularly during sex. More commonly called the "love hormone," it is released at the height of climax, where it builds up, creates an explosion, and the brain is overwhelmed with the sensation from oxytocin overload. It's no wonder most people confuse orgasms with love because that explosion feels so fucking good.

Sex and love are not related. The only relationship that exists between sex and love is the one you create in your mind. It is possible to have sex, enjoy it immensely, and walk away with no other feeling besides *"damn, that ass was good!"* You don't love that person. The individual just made you feel good when you needed it most. For those who've cheated in their relationships, you know exactly what I mean. You can love your partner to death and still have amazing sex with another, and yet another, but you still love the one you love. The difference between men and women is that most men have the innate ability to compartmentalize sex and love. They seem to understand that sex is an act that can occur in absence of love, while love is feelings and emotions that can occur in absence of sex. Thus, men find it easier to separate the women they love from the women they fuck. Women, on the other hand, continue to struggle with this notion. When a woman finds out her man is cheating, one of the first questions she asks is *"do you love her?"* Rarely does she ask if the pussy was better than hers because she thinks his cheating has something to do with his emotions, not about the sex. At the same time, she feels as if he's lied about loving her because *"how can he love me and fuck someone else?"* The reality is that it's easy for him to fuck other women because he simply wants to feel the insides of different pussy, and being in a monogamous relationship, doesn't allow him to do that. When he cheats, love typically has little to do with it. It doesn't matter how good a woman fucks or feeds her man; he will eventually want some other pussy. Some men may not act on it, but most (dare I say all) men think about fucking someone else besides their partner. But here's something else men need to think about; all women aren't content with just one dick. That same idea of "newness" that men chase resonates within women as well. It's just that some women have a harder time separating sex from love due to the conditioning and brainwashing they were subjected to since childhood. This is a difficult notion for some men to understand because they are ego-driven and often insecure. What most men don't realize is that women get bored of getting the same dick day in and day out too. I happen to be such a woman, and although people tend to think I am a rare breed for thinking that way, I believe the rarity is only in that I verbalize and act upon it, while most women are too afraid to do either. It is a part of the human condition to want change and variety in almost everything we do, and sex is no exception. As the pioneer of sex research, Alfred Kinsey, put it, "*The only universal in human sexuality is variability itself.*" Variety is the spice of life, and without it, life is fifty shades of *boring*.

Men do not view sex as love. I feel like this concept is worthy of repeating again and again. Marvin Gay, one of the sexiest Black men to create sensual music about sex and love, said it best during a 1983 interview with radio host, Tom Joyner:

> **Tom**: *How do you feel about love?*
>
> **Marvin**: *Love is misery (laughs). Love is miserable. I think I'll be a bachelor and I'll swing, and I won't fall in love. I'll just be love-full. Be kind and good, and have fun. I don't feel like being miserable.*
>
> **Tom**: *Marriage?*
>
> **Marvin**: *Miserable. (Tom laughs) Miserable. Except if you find the right one that's your soulmate, and that takes a lot of looking. Um... I'll never marry again until I know I'm ready and that I have the right lady and the right consciousness. And a good girl. A girl who don't fool around too much and all that stuff.*

Tom: Sex.

Marvin: *Sex? Oh god! Sex is marvelous.*

Tom: *Love is miserable. Marriage is miserable and…*

Marvin: *Sex is great. (Tom laughs). Yeah, that's about right for me right now. You know there is quite a separation between the two as far as I'm concerned. I think that sex is really sex and love is love. If you happen to love the person you're having sex with, that's tremendous, but I really see a complete separation, and the two are totally unrelated to me.[4]*

Marvin's words resonated with me, as I'm sure they do with most men and others who are non-monogamous. Not that love and marriage are miserable, but that sex and love are two separate things. Women who don't share this sentiment are headed into situations they are ill-prepared for when they believe that sex and love are the same and enter into relationships with men who see the two as unrelated.

The separation of sex and love in my mind happened later in life, so I completely understand how most women feel. I was raised to believe that polygamy was normal as a Muslim girl. Yet, I still wanted to experience love in monogamous relationships because society said that monogamy was normal. When I was cheated on, I would be so devastated because I thought his heart was for another woman. I couldn't understand how someone I loved could have sex with someone else. I was too wrapped up in my own feelings to see that he was just fulfilling his desire to enjoy sex with other women. I am not holding a torch for cheating men or their behavior. I'm merely stating that I understand why the cheating happened. I realize now that the sex he had with other women was not a degradation of his love for me; it was him tapping into his sexual nature because we were living the monogamous lie. As I evolved into a more mature and open-minded woman, I don't view cheating as I once did. Cheating to me is more about lies, deceit, and disloyalty, and much less about sex. I believe that once you're able to separate love from sex, it will be easier to accept that both you and your partner can love one another while sharing each other with other people and possibly eliminate the need to cheat at all.

Sex and religion shouldn't be used in the same sentence let alone combining them together to determine what you should do in your bedroom. With its strict rules and level of control over people's behaviors, religion destroyed the fun and enjoyment we find in sex. It also has everything to do with the sex/love attachment that is so hard to unlearn due to its anti-premarital (before marriage) and anti-extramarital (outside of marriage) rhetoric[5]; sex before marriage is a sin, sex with others besides your husband or wife is a sin, sex is a gift from God, sex within marriage is sacred....I could go on and on but I think you catch my drift. For quite some time, sex was considered dirty and taboo, something that couldn't be talked about and should only be experienced between husband and wife. Although many of us view sex quite differently today, the connection between love and sex remains. Unfortunately, people are embarrassed to be honest about their sexuality because religion turned them away from the enjoyment we all find in sex. The shame and guilt you feel when fantasizing about threesomes, orgies, or just giving head to a stranger are deeply rooted in religious beliefs and sex-negativity. Those are the same negative feelings that keep so many of you in unhappy, miserable, and sexless relationships. Your value, self-worth, or access to spirituality are not determined by who you have sex with. And I doubt very seriously that God cares about how often you have sex or whom you enjoy it with.

Having permissible sex outside of your relationship is not a sin, nor is it wrong. It is possible for you and your partner to maintain your loving relationship while having the freedom to explore and fulfill your needs with others. Don't think for a moment that your lust-filled thoughts for different people make you a sinner or a whore. That's just what society wants you to believe. Accepting those desires within makes you as normal as the heart beating in your chest. The love you have for each other should not change if your love is strong, and your relationship will remain intact if both partners are on the same page. It's okay to stop lying to yourself and pretending you are content with fucking just one person for the rest of your life. I have already accepted that reality; now's *your turn*.

IT'S THE SEX ENERGY FOR ME!

"Sex energy isn't visible but it is always present."

S ex energy is the driving force of your life, whether you're willing to accept it or not. That doesn't mean that sex is the only reason we exist, although, without sex, none of us would be here. Sex energy is present before, during, and long after physical contact ends. That deep thump between your legs, the carnal desire that captivates your every thought when reflecting on a particular person or situation, the spark that is created when you make contact with the one that makes your mouth water, your dick hard, or your pussy wet- *that* is sex energy. When a good-looking man or woman walks past you and smiles, and you smile back and blush, you've exchanged sex energy. Sex energy isn't visible, but it is always present. You may not always be conscious of its presence until it is ignited by a thought, a fragrance, or a particular sound, but we exchange sex energy all day long. You don't have to be in the presence of the individual(s) for the exchange to happen, but when you meet someone whose sex energy matches yours, the connection is undeniable.

All sex energy is not created equally. The sex energy of a person can vary from high to low and can be the reason why a sexual encounter is incredible or the cause of an absolute disaster. An individual can exist at any point on that spectrum, but the level of sexual compatibility between individuals depends on where they meet on the spectrum. If you have high sex energy, it will be difficult for you to find ultimate pleasure in a low sex energy person. I'm quite sure you've had sex with someone whose sex energy didn't match yours, and once it was done, you labeled the person a dead fuck. Although an attraction can exist between the two, the low sex energy person will lack what it takes to keep the spark lit. This quickly leads to boredom or displeasure in the high sex energy partner.

I have high sex energy, and having sex with a person who has low sex energy, bores the fuck out of me. In the past, I didn't consider the importance of sex energy. I would just have sex with men that I was attracted to. If the sex was bad, I would chalk it up to incompatibility or interpret the lack of enthusiasm to mean a lack of interest in me. But once I locked into the idea of matching sexual energies, I started to realize that I rarely enjoyed sex with low sex energy people. If it's a person I have a strong desire to fuck, I often try to understand where that person is sexually. I'll ask how often he/she thinks about sex or how often they feel the need to have sex. You'd be surprised how many people have very low sex energy or a decreased desire for sex in general. These kinds of people are useless to me when I want to have my sexual needs met. I have high sex energy, and I must have high sex energy partners. Understanding the differences in sex energies became more vital to me as I fucked more single men, began engaging in sex with couples and participating in orgies.

I once met a really sexy Black couple through another couple I engaged in sex with from time to time. We met briefly while attending a Lifestyle club in Atlanta. The woman was gorgeous, pretty face, full lips, and a fat ass. She was with her man, who was also attractive, but, like before, I was more interested in the energy between her and me. She had an infectious, flirty demeanor, which immediately made me aware of her interest in me. The night was ending, but I already had plans, so we agreed to hook up at another time. A few months later, I was returning to Atlanta, so the three of us decided to meet up for lunch to see if we could catch a vibe. While we ate and talked, I could feel the subtle anxiety from the unknown. I really wanted to have an amazing experience and was becoming eager to find out if things would turn out that way. I could feel the moistness building between my thighs as I realized she was also very interested to see how things would play out. She touched me frequently and gave me the flirty smile I love to see on a woman's face when she looks at me.

When we got back to the hotel, she and I decided to take a shower together to help break the ice. While in the shower, I lathered up a washcloth and began washing her body. I kissed her neck, her nipples then squatted down low to place my mouth between her legs. I'm always very eager to get to the pussy, to smell it and taste it. Our energies were harmonizing, and as I started to lick and suck her, she moaned and grabbed my hair, letting me know that she enjoyed it and wanted more. As I continued to suck her sweetness, her man stood in the bathroom doorway, watching and stroking his dick, waiting for his opportunity to join us.

When we exited the shower, she pushed me onto the bed, spread my legs, and started sucking my pussy. He kneeled over me and slid his dick into my mouth. We continued for a bit, but he made it known that he wanted to taste me. She got up, and he slid down between my legs to exchange places with her. I turned over and spread my legs for him to lick me from behind. I slid her beneath me so her pussy was right above my chin. As I licked her, he became impatient and wanted to feel me. He put on a condom, and as he slid inside me, I could feel the gush as my pussy wrapped around his dick. I moaned loudly. His package was how I liked it, thick, long, and hard. While he fucked me, I sucked her fat, sweet pussy. My blood ran hot. I loved to get a good dick down with a juicy, pretty pussy in my mouth. The sex energy between us was intoxicating. She squirmed and wrapped her fingers in my sister locs. He dug deeper and deeper inside me as I tried to suck her pussy dry. I was loving that shit and didn't want to stop, but I wanted to watch him fuck her. I slid my body upwards, kissing her nipples then her mouth, letting her have a taste of her own juices. As I crawled up to sit my pussy on her face, he slid inside her and immediately started to dick her down good. She struggled beneath the weight of us both but let out loud moans with every thrust he made. I strategically placed my pussy on her mouth so that she could lick and moan at the same time. As I turned to face him, he let me know he was ready to be inside me again. After he pulled out of her I leaned in to suck her juices from his dick. His body immediately responded as his erection became firmer. I knew he was ready for me. I laid face down, ass up and he only paused long enough to slide on a condom before entering me once more. While he fucked me, she sucked my nipples and cheered him on. She kept saying, "Fuck that pussy good, baby," and "Yes, baby, give her that good dick." The more she cheered him on, the closer I was to climaxing. There's nothing sexier than a bad bitch cheering her man on while he finds pleasure in pleasing another woman.

After I came, he climbed on top of her, and I returned the favor. I told him how good the dick was, and how badly I wanted him to make her cum. I sucked her nipples and rubbed her clit as he pounded her. After she came, he *pulled out and let loose, all over her belly. The three of us were exhausted, and after another hot shower, we retired for the night.*

The next morning, we started over again. She and I pleased one another in the shower, taking turns licking and washing each other. I wanted more dick but she wanted more time to wash. When I got out, he was sitting in the chair looking through his phone. I walked over to him, wet and wanting. I dropped to my knees and sucked his dick until he achieved the appropriate hardness. As he slid the condom on, I climbed on top and rode him like a bull. As I spun around so he could hit it from the back, I noticed her watching us from the bathroom doorway. Watching her pleasing facial expressions while I rode her man made me cum loud and hard. After I came, she yelled out, "Yes, baby! Get all that pussy!" Needless to say, it was an amazing time.

This is what I mean when I refer to sex energies that match. She was energetic as fuck! Her active and assertive participation kept me turned on, which increased my naturally high sex energy level. Fucking a couple or more than one person at a time takes a lot of energy. When the sex energies are compatible, the sexual experience is immensely more pleasurable. As you and your partner begin to explore sex with other women or couples, you will find the level of sex energy that is appealing to you. Depending on the situation, it may be up to you to keep the session exciting by ramping up your sex energy.

Whether you're having sex with an individual or sharing your partner during a session, you need to understand your sex energy level and those of the others involved. The last thing you want to do is invite others into your bed when you have no idea if your energies match. However, this isn't always easy to establish. In highly erogenous environments, it is easy to become consumed by all of the sex energy in that space, leading you to think a person or couple is more sexual than they actually are. Of course, you will meet people and feel the energy immediately, but, oftentimes, people are slow to reveal their true sexual natures. You also may be surprised to find that the one you're most attracted to, has sex energy that isn't like yours at all.

Sex energy plays a huge role in how you relate to others sexually. However, understanding how you identify your sexuality is also vital to enjoying the pleasures the Lifestyle has to offer. Are you a straight couple only interested in having sex with the opposite genders? Or are you a bi female with a straight male, only interested in other women for both of you? Regardless of your interests, you must identify who you are as a sexual being to find playmates that can provide you with the delights you fantasize about. These are just a couple of options available for you to connect with, but keep in mind that who you are and how you begin as a Lifestyler can change and evolve over time. Don't get discouraged if all of this is new to you. You may not have the slightest idea what you actually like or who you are sexually. Most people are probably in the exact space you occupy now, and that's okay. Now is the time for you to start working through the thoughts and feelings you have as you begin your Lifestyle journey. The next step is learning and understanding what it means to be in the Lifestyle.

LIFESTYLE 101

"You don't have to pick just one person and be stuck with that one forever."

What does it mean to be in the Lifestyle? The Lifestyle, or LS, is an umbrella term used to describe the practice of individuals who do not believe in traditional monogamy. Instead, they participate in non-monogamous sex and relationships. Non-monogamy is at the heart of the Lifestyle community. There is no right or wrong way to Lifestyle as long as the people involved are cognizant and consenting adults. You may have heard of the terms ethical non-monogamy or consensual non-monogamy, which basically means all partners are on board with sex and/or relationships with others. Traditionally, the parties involved have decided that monogamy, or sex with one person, would not make them happy and have chosen to create a life outside of the monogamy box, which they've found to be more fulfilling. Some enter the Lifestyle solely to enhance their sex lives, seeking sexual gratification from other single individuals or couples with similar sexual interests. The purpose is to create more memorable sexual experiences without strings or commitments; commonly known as swinging. While others are looking for short or long-term relationships with multiple individuals or other couples for, not only sex, but love, companionship, tribe building, or other like-minded people just to have fun with; more commonly known as poly. There are many ways of relating to one another in the Lifestyle. Therefore, when you choose this way of life, you get to be the writer of the pages of your book and create the kind of relationships you want to be in. If you are already in a relationship, you and your partner get to decide what works for both of you, then you can create another version of your existing relationship that makes you happy.

If the term Lifestyle is new to you, don't worry. It is not a common subject you will hear talked about in coffee shops or book clubs. It is generally whispered about amongst those introduced to some aspect of the Lifestyle, but it is kept secret until the environment is deemed safe and non-judgmental. Perhaps you have a friend that has some experience with threesomes or participated in an orgy or two. You may have even been invited home by a couple who thought you would make a nice third to their duo. If you listened to the friend's stories or participated in the advancement by the couple, that was your introduction to the Lifestyle. I'm sure you've heard of terms like polyamory, polygamy, swingers, friends with benefits, and open relationships. Each of these non-monogamous relationship types, which will be discussed in more detail later in the book, are different but fall under the Lifestyle umbrella. There isn't a rule that says you can only be one type or another. You and your partner can decide which relationship style suits your sexual or emotional needs, bearing in mind those needs may change in the future. The idea is to be open to things that are different than what you may have been taught or gravitated to in adulthood simply because it's all you know.

In the Lifestyle, you can enjoy more sexual and emotional freedom, rather than tailoring your needs around religious morals and beliefs, that end up leaving you unsatisfied and unhappy. You gravitated to this book because something about non-monogamy piqued your interest. Or maybe you were just curious to know who in the hell would have the audacity to say FUCK Monogamy out loud. Either way, this guidebook will help you understand what it means to be in the Lifestyle and may ultimately help bring more satisfaction to your relationship. This satisfaction can come in different forms, but you get to choose what is right for you. You will learn that in the Lifestyle, you don't have to pick just one person and be stuck with that one forever. Now, if monogamy works for you, great! By all means, carry on. But if you seek sexual freedom and/or emotional and loving connections with other people besides your partner, cast your fears and judgments aside and read on.

Since this is Lifestyle 101, I want to take a moment to introduce you to some basic Lifestyle (LS) terminology. In the LS, almost everything has an acronym or nickname. It really has its own language. In this book, I'll use a few of the more common terms, but, trust me, there are hundreds. Here's a crash course of basic LS phrases and labels to help you get more acquainted. You can use this as a guide to help you understand this text as you read further. Given that this is just an entry-level list, I'll keep it short and sweet.

LS = Lifestyle

Lifestyler = A person in the Lifestyle

Vanilla = Non-lifestyle (Could be a person or situation)

Monogamist = A person who only wants to have a sexual and emotional relationship with one partner

Monogamish = A person who is not really poly, but not 100% closed to having other partners

Non-monogamist = A person who does not have, nor want, a relationship, sexual or otherwise, with just one partner

Polyamory = Having multiple sexual or loving relationships

Polygamy = Having more than one wife or husband at the same time

Polygany = Man having more than one wife

Polyandry = Woman having more than one husband

Solo Poly = A person who identifies as poly but does not identify very strongly as a part of a couple and prefers to operate as an individual

Swingers = Couples seeking sex with other couples or singles

Open relationship = This term varies but usually means both partners can seek and have sex and/or emotional attachments outside of the relationship

Relationship Anarchy = Partners are free to engage in any relationships they choose at any time

Metamour = The lover of a partner who the other partner has no relationship with

Paramour = A lover outside of the relationship

Hierarchy = Relationships based on levels of seniority

Primary, Secondary, Tertiary partner = Refers to level of authority and/or priority in hierarchical relationships

Polyfidelity = Refers to a relationship that involves two or more people who don't permit relationships with additional partners without everyone's approval

Compersion = The opposite of jealousy. When a partner experiences pleasure or joy from their partner's joy in another relationship.

Threesome = Refers to sex with three participants

Foursome = Refers to sex with four participants

Moresome = Refers to group sex or orgy with five or more participants

Full Swap = Both male and female in a couple have oral and penetrative sex with another couple

Soft Swap = Male and /or Female in a couple only participates in heavy petting or oral sex with the other couples or singles, no penetration allowed

Voyeur = One who gets off by watching others have sex

MFM = Male Female Male (threesome where the woman is the center of attention and the males don't have sexual contact)

FMF = Female Male Female (opposite of MFM)

MMF = Male Male Female (threesome where the males have sexual contact with each other and the female)

FFM = Female Female Male (opposite of MMF)

MFMF = Foursome that is full swap non-bisexual contact

MMFF = Foursome where all participants have bi play with each other

MFFM = Foursome where females have bi play

FMMF = Foursome where males have bi play

BBW = Big Black Woman or Big Beautiful Woman

SBW = Single Black Woman

BBM = Big Black Male

FWB = Friends with benefits

HWP = Height and Weight Proportionate (This refers to those who aren't overweight, obese, or super slim)

BBC = Big Black Cock

BBD = Big Black Dick

Chode = Short fat dick

Fluid-bonding = The choice partners make to not use barrier protection, which usually coincides with an agreement to have protected sex with others and regular STI testing

Bareback = No condom or barrier protection (Applies to oral as well)

Unicorn = A single bisexual woman who enjoys sex with couples

Bull = A single male who has sex with couples (Straight or bi)

Fuckability = How fuckable a person is on a scale of 1-10

Play = Any sexual contact

Playdate = Time set aside to entertain sex with others

DP = Double Penetration (A woman fucking two men at the same time with one in the pink, and one in the stink)

Cuckhold = A man who finds pleasure in watching his woman fuck other men

DnD free = Drug and disease free

BFE/GFE = Boyfriend or Girlfriend Experience

NRE = New relationship energy

This is just a short list of terms that will be useful for you to know as you begin your Lifestyle journey. Once you start seeking other LS people and going to different LS events, you need to be able to communicate your needs and boundaries to others. As I said, there are hundreds more, but these are enough to keep you from looking like an ass when you mistake BBD to mean the R&B group, instead of the Big Black Dick you just signed up for.

THE LIFESTYLE'S LACK
OF BLACKNESS

"That's White people's shit."

My experience in the Lifestyle as a Black woman is vastly different than those of White women. As I discovered my sexuality, I searched for guidance from other highly sexual women like myself, hoping to gain some perspective regarding non-monogamy. I read books and watched videos about women who did not find satisfaction with monogamous sex because, like me, they found it boring and monotonous. The only problem was that none of those women, with so much profound knowledge to share, looked like me. As I read about some of their experiences, I was having a hard time relating. As I attended more Lifestyle events, I rarely saw people who looked like me or met other Black people who thought about relationships the way I did. In the past six years, every Lifestyle convention, social club, or event I have ever gone to was predominantly White. Go to Hedonism II, the biggest Lifestyle resort in the Caribbean, on an average week that isn't "Black Week," and you'll primarily see White folks with a sprinkle of chocolate here and there. As I navigated more into the world of non-monogamy, I realized there was very little Black presence in the Lifestyle, at least publicly. That revelation spoke volumes to me, which led me to dig deeper into why people of color rarely participated in Lifestyle events and created my desire to enlighten Black folks about non-monogamy and Lifestyle culture. What I discovered is that most Black people believe that the Lifestyle is for White people. We've misguidedly associated certain behaviors like partying nude or swinging to Whiteness, when in fact, the things we commonly refer to as "White people's shit" is shit we actually enjoy doing but are too ashamed to admit.

Don't be fooled; Black people love to do "White people's shit." When I attend LS "friendly" events that are predominantly Black, I bear witness to Black people doing all the things they say Black folks don't do. Black folks enjoy partying nude. We love to fuck in rooms full of people and enjoy swapping partners with other couples. We have parties, we swing, we dance and we fuck. The problem is, Black people prefer to do these things in the dark, which generates not only a negative attitude or stigma around those behaviors, it also creates a barrier for other Black people to embrace the culture and accept that the Lifestyle could lead to a higher quality of life.

What the fuck is "White people's shit" anyway? The notion that certain behaviors are for White people and Black folks should not partake in them is asinine, especially as it pertains to sex and sexuality. White people don't own the rights to pleasure and sexual fulfillment, nor do they claim to. It's Black folks' lack of engagement in Lifestyle environments and activities that keep them predominantly White. When I have this conversation with them they say, "When I go to a nude beach there's mostly old, overweight, and horny White people walking around." Well, how can we expect anything more if we don't patronize these environments? As I continued exploring the reasons for the lack of diversity in the Lifestyle, I realized that Black folks didn't choose not to engage in the Lifestyle because it wasn't for them; they choose not to openly partake in the Lifestyle out of fear. The sad part is that this fear is self-generated because they are afraid of being scrutinized and judged by others who have little or nothing to do with their happiness. This statement is so integral to understanding why it takes us so long to progress, that it bears repeating. Black folks fear the scrutiny and judgment from others who have little or nothing to do with their happiness.

Fear is one hell of a motivator. It will influence an individual's choice to do things that he/she wouldn't do otherwise. In this instance, both Black men and women choose to avoid the Lifestyle out of fear of being seen as less than "normal." Most of us are already afraid of being any more different than our skin makes us, so we've limited any unnecessary exposure to those environments. Because the Lifestyle isn't considered "normal," we shy away from it, label it "White people's shit" to spare ourselves the embarrassment for enjoying it, and then secretly participate in it to avoid being judged.

The fears that Black folks have about the Lifestyle have been bred from cultural attitudes and societal norms that were forced upon us for centuries. When I reflect on my experiences with Black men in situations involving nudity and sex, I realize they are reluctant to participate in activities that may place their manhood into question. The fear of appearing less than manly renders them incapable of transforming into carefree individuals without certain assurances, in particular, whatever happens, must remain a secret. On the other hand, Black women who want to be viewed as "wifey" material, will avoid activity that would instead lead men to label them whores, sluts, fast, or any of the other derogatory names chosen for women who don't conform to the "virgin" ideology. From my explorations, I've determined there are four major fears that exist in the hearts and minds of Black people that prevent them from openly embracing Lifestyle culture and seeing the potential benefits non-monogamy could have on their relationships.

1. **Black people can't let go of the shame associated with nudity.**

   During my explorations, I found that six out of ten Black men had never been naked in public nor desired to be. They were extremely uncomfortable with the thought of being exposed around strangers; who would see them, who they would tell, and what they would say. When asked why they had such apprehension about public nudity, the first response is, "that's White people shit." This is ironic, considering nudity was common in the African culture *before* the slave trade and religion fucked it all up.

   Black people have been heavily influenced by Christian culture since slavery. To be clear; when they stole us, we were naked and we were happy. When they landed in the "Americas", we were naked and we were content. Our nudity was natural, not sexual. But they shamed us into feeling the opposite and now the thought of being naked in front of people embarrasses us. Nudity is our most natural state regardless of race. Jewels, traditional cloth, and body tattoos were typically worn as adornments to display wealth and prestige, not as coverings for our "private parts." However, once Christian beliefs associated nudity with shame and sin, (you know; the whole Adam and Eve story), wearing clothing or garments to cover the body became commonplace.

There was a time when nudity was associated with the perfection of the Gods, and the body's exposure was customary. But once White colonizers came upon us in our native lands, they forced us into slavery and clothing, shamed us into thinking nakedness was lewd and sinful, then turned around and established nude "baths", beaches, and colonies for Whites to appreciate. We were browbeaten to believe nudity was for the uncivilized and low class, but now White folks use nudity as a symbol of non-conformity and free expression. This is an example of "White privilege." They make the rules for everyone to follow but break them whenever it suits them.

To this day, Black folks still don't feel comfortable walking around nude, even in our own homes. We are ashamed of our hair, our skin, and our gorgeous bodies. Only recently have Black men and women been considered "the sexiest alive," but that's still according to White standards. White people have been force-feeding us their perception of beauty for centuries. Because of this, we find it difficult to embrace the beauty in our Blackness. The over-sexualization of Black women in television, music, and videos helps perpetuate the body negativity so many of us endure. We shy away from environments where our bodies are on display for others to see, so it is uncommon to see Black people on nude beaches or at events that involve nudity.

2. **Black men tend to be homophobic.**

Everything is "gay". A threesome with a woman and another man; gay. Even when there is no guy-on-guy contact; gay. Going to a nude beach, hanging out in a nude pool, or being in any environment where other dicks are exposed, is gay. Even watching porn with a man penetrating a woman may be considered gay because the man watching gets aroused from looking at another man's dick enter a pussy. (This one confused the hell out of me, but a Black man actually said this to me.) Now woman-on-woman contact is okay, but the idea of being naked or engaging in sexual acts while another man is present is an easy pass for most Black men because it could be seen as gay behavior or having gay tendencies. To many of them, there's nothing worse than being labeled "gay", when you aren't.

What's wrong with being gay? Again, slavery and religion play huge roles in modern Black culture. They have everything to do with how we see ourselves and what we deem appropriate or acceptable. In Christianity and Islam, being gay is still considered an abomination, and those who are staunch believers in their faith will never accept gayness as a form of "normal" sexuality. Black gay men, in particular, continue to struggle for acceptance even amongst the LBGTQ+ community, and, although being gay is more acceptable in society today, straight Black men don't want to be seen as gay, due to the homonegativity that is attached to it. Right or wrong, homophobia is so deeply rooted in the Black community that it prevents Black men from participating in acts that could place their manhood into question.

In Lifestyle situations, it's common to have two or more dicks in any given space. But the thought of seeing another man's dick or potentially touching another man during sex is enough to make the hardest Black dick limp. Black men say things like "I don't want to touch a man when I'm fucking", or "I don't want my nuts around no other man's nuts," which is enough to keep them away from environments where there is any chance of coming in contact with another man. That kind of thinking has minimized the quality and quantity of available Black men and Black couples in the Lifestyle in general. This is a shame because I thoroughly enjoy being the third to sexy Black couples desiring to share their sex with me. However, there is usually only a minimal number of available couples willing to play at major LS events because the men are afraid of what people may think if they find out where they go to look for sex. What these men fail to realize is that the majority of men in the Lifestyle are straight men looking for pussy, and more pussy. They are looking to find female playmates for themselves and their partners, to participate in orgies of various sizes, or becoming a third to a couple in a cuckold, where they fuck another man's woman while he watches. Nothing about any of that is gay, nor is it just "White people's shit." This ignorant kind of thinking has also made it very difficult for women like me to find two Black men who are interested in double penetration sex. It's relatively easy to find two White men ready to double-dip into my chocolatey goodness any day of the week. However, trying to find two Black men, especially two who don't know each other, to DP me is rare. They simply cannot accept the presence of another man's dick. But how can two straight men, giving a woman the ultimate pleasure, be considered gay? It's bullshit notions like these that keep the Lifestyle from becoming more diverse, and me from getting thoroughly fucked.

3. **A Black man is the least likely to allow another man to penetrate his woman.**

The fear of his woman enjoying the dick of another man is enough to drive him insane. Plenty of Black men are okay with sharing their women with other women, because, toy or no toy, women don't have dicks, so there's no conflict. But it is inconceivable for those same men to share their women with other men. Forget about it! Most Black men will not stand by while another man dicks their woman down. They'd die first! This, I believe, stops a lot of Black men from entering the Lifestyle or at least restructuring their monogamous relationship into a non-monogamous one; they'd rather keep cheating. I see it all of the time, single Black men roaming around at LS-friendly events, ready to fuck someone else's woman, but rarely bringing pussy of their own into that environment to share with others. Black men rarely like to share pussy they think is theirs because they see women as their property and treat them as possessions.

It's no secret that women didn't have rights at one point in time and were deemed property for men to do with as they pleased. Sounds familiar, right? A lot like slavery? But even with the abolishment of slavery, with it being inhumane and all, men refuse to let go of the idea that women belong to them. For reasons that are so deeply ingrained from past trauma, Black men tend to hold more value over the idea that their woman is their property and untouchable by others. They expect women to accept that they have an inherent need to be pleased by multiple women, however what pleases her isn't considered if it meant another man would be responsible for it. Their egos become deflated at the thought of another man pleasing their woman differently or even better than them.

Conversely, men from other cultures do not regard this idea of "untouchableness" as high. As a matter of fact, a White man will *specifically* seek out Black men with big dicks, to fuck his woman. He *likes* to watch his woman get a good dicking because he knows it brings her pleasure. He also knows she's not leaving him for some dick, no matter how good it is, if she's happy in the relationship. So, he's willing to gift her something he can't provide: a Big Black Cock. A happy wife is a happy life, at least that's what they say. It's about time that Black men understand that their dicks are not golden, and new dick to women feels the same as new pussy to them.

4. **Single Black women fear not being accepted by men, so they aren't likely to acknowledge they want to be non-monogamous.**

Everyone knows that men hold the key to relationships and marriage. A woman is not in a relationship or getting married to a man if he doesn't choose her, claims her, or asks for her hand in marriage. Therefore, most women wouldn't acknowledge their desire to be with more than one man because they risk losing a potential mate, especially if that man only wants to be in a monogamous relationship. Black women, particularly those who prefer to be with Black men, have a much smaller pool of quality men to choose from, so they are *even less* likely to openly admit their desire to have more than one dick in their lives.

After probing into this theory further, I realized that lots of women desire to fuck more than one man. However, the sex-negativity that plagues this society, especially as it relates to a woman's vagina, forces women to repress their sexual desires to maintain the misogynistic views of how a woman should behave. A Black woman won't go to a place like Hedonism alone if it means putting her pussy on trial. Lord knows men are still out here counting the number of bodies a woman fucks and handing out guilty verdicts based on their ideas of what being a "ho" means to them. Recently, a man who sees himself as a "high-quality man" told me that *"the man is the prize"* and that *"a woman is only good for some pussy and her ability to have kids."* If men really think that way, women can never feel free to be out here in these streets fucking as men do because the more sex they have, the lower their stock, and the lower their value is to a man. It's foolishness. Yet, when you consider that a Black woman has limited options in terms of finding a compatible Black man of "quality", she is not going to risk being seen as loose. This is especially true when her end game is to be in a relationship with a man who otherwise has many options.

There needs to be a culture shift led by both Black men and women to change the demographic of the Lifestyle. The men can take the lead by no longer equating a woman's value by how close to a virgin she is, and understand that she is human with similar needs as his that deserve recognition. The women need to stop placing the value of a relationship with a man higher than the value of her own emotional and sexual well-being and liberate herself. Black women will not be forthcoming about what they truly desire until men stop devaluing a woman's needs in order to fit antiquated and outdated ways of thinking about how a woman should behave. Plain and simple.

We must stop saying that non-monogamy and alternative relationship styles are for White people. Going to a nude beach or inviting friends over to party naked is not just for White people. Inviting a sexy woman into your bed for you and your partner to share is not just for White people. Yes, White people are probably more inclined to do these things, but that's because they are more open about their shit and collectively find ways to get it.

The lack of Blackness in LS environments is our fault. All of this shit is for us if we stop giving a fuck about how other people see us and just live. If we want the Lifestyle to be more diverse, then we need to diversify it. Most LS environments cater to White people because they are the dominant patrons, so there's little need to be concerned about the Black experience. But there is a place for Black people if we are willing to live outside the little boxes we've placed ourselves in. We don't need to be so private about our involvement in non-monogamous relationships. There's this inherent thought of *"I don't want anyone to know"* that keeps us from living sexually uninhibited lives. Being sexually free is a great thing. Why keep that locked away? I get that there needs to be some level of discretion because of the judgmental attitudes of monogamous people and the risk of losing personal or business relationships. However, we can't continue to complain about what isn't available to us if we aren't consistently supporting and/or creating LS environments of our own. Most White folks don't give a damn what people think. They do whatever the fuck they want. We need to move with that same energy.

TO BI OR NOT TO BI

**"I thought I was strictly dickly, until
I tasted my friend's pussy."**

I licked my first pussy when I was twenty-five. She and I had been friends since high school and began creating a stronger bond as grown women. We were getting really close, but I had never considered anything sexual happening between us. I had been around plenty of women most of my life and never felt sexual desire for any of them. But on this particular Friday night, things changed. She and I were hanging out and bar hopping in the streets of Philly. I had on a tiny white miniskirt with no panties, which was normal for me. As I drove to the next location, we chatted and sang songs. Suddenly, she placed her hand on my leg and started rubbing my knee. For whatever reason, I didn't freeze. I remember glancing down at her hand and then over to her, but she was staring out the passenger window. As I continued to drive, she started moving her hand up my thigh then between my legs. I recall thinking, "Wait…What's happening here?" But this time, I didn't look over at her. I don't know if she looked at me, but she slowly slid her pinky between the lips of my pussy. I responded as anyone would; I opened my legs wider and slid my ass down a bit in the seat. With better access, she slid more fingers over and began rubbing my pussy softly. At that time, I wasn't sure what was happening, but the freak in me wanted to figure it out. I remember we stopped at a bar to see if it was open. She got out of the car to check, and when she did, I called a guy friend of mine and told him what was happening. He just said he wished he could be there and told me to go for it. So, I said, "Fuck it! I'll do it!" Liquid courage needed to be my wingman that night so I made sure we had access to more drinks. I never imagined that I would be sexually interested in a woman. Women had come onto me before, but I always shut them down quickly because I was strictly dickly. That was my favorite go-to line, but I didn't use it on this particular night. She was a baddie. I really liked her as a friend, but I had never felt attracted to her. Yet, when she touched me, it didn't feel weird or disgusting. I was actually intrigued and curious to see how far things would go. I wasn't sure if I could eat pussy, but my curiosity was definitely stronger than my belief that I was a girl who only liked dick.

We must've hit up two more bars before deciding we were lit enough to head home. As we drank, we didn't talk about her touching me earlier in the car. We just acted as if everything was normal. I was grateful for the alcohol because I needed the liquid courage to go through what was about to happen. I ended up drinking too much, so she had to drive us home. When we pulled up to her place, she leaned over, popped my seat back, spread my thighs, and started licking my pussy. I propped my legs back so that her tongue could run smoothly between my flesh. To my surprise, it felt really good. However, back then, even when I had sex with men, licking me was a must. So, transitioning that into a sexy chick doing the same was not so difficult, friend or not. She licked and sucked my pussy for a few minutes, but, eventually, our position wasn't working, so we headed into her apartment. Once we entered her room, I laid down, and she continued to eat me out. Although it felt good, it wasn't great, and I wanted it to be better. Later, I found out it was her first time too. I stopped her after a while and said, "Let me show you how I like it." I wanted to please her how I wanted to be pleased but I also wanted to take a chance and get a little taste of my own. We switched places, and I immediately started licking her how I liked to be licked. As I listened to her moan, I felt good about what I was doing, although it was also my first time. She tasted sweet and a little salty, but her pussy was fresh. The more I licked her, the more I wanted her to cum, but here's where it got a bit tricky. A part of my aversion to sex with women was I knew how unclean a vagina could be. I lived with many women, dormitory-style, so I knew that women could be some nasty asses. I also knew what it took to keep mine fresh and clean, so I never wanted to discover what was on the inside of another woman's vagina. Yet, that night, I felt adventurous.

As she moaned and grabbed the back of my head, I slid two fingers inside her. As she tried to pull away, I summoned her back with my tongue while keeping my fingers deep inside and was reluctant to pull my fingers out. Not because I didn't want to. It was because my biggest fear with pussy, in general, was the thought of what I could potentially withdraw from that hole if it wasn't clean inside. But once I inserted my fingers into her, she moaned so lovely that I had to keep going. I kept my fingers in deep, moving them as little as possible so I wouldn't get any of her inner juices on my tongue. Yeah, I was being a punk but I had already gone so far that there was no turning back. I continued to lick and suck and lick and suck and fingered her until she came. After she came, I continued to lick her softly; the scent of her orgasmic juices made my head spin. As I was silently gloating and feeling impressed with myself, it suddenly occurred to me, "What am I going to pull out of her pussy when I take my fingers out?" Maybe the thought made me nauseous, or *perhaps it was the alcohol, but when I pulled my fingers out, a sudden rush of dizziness took hold of me. I stumbled from the room and quickly made it to the bathroom, where I puked my brains out. Then I passed out on her cold-ass bathroom floor. After that night, we didn't speak about it for many years, although we remained the closest of friends. It would be almost seven years before I had a sexual encounter with another woman.*

If you're a woman and you've never considered being with a woman sexually, you're probably grossed out. I get it. Girl-on-girl play is not your thing. However, although not a requirement for non-monogamous relationships, women having sex with other women is a major part of the Lifestyle. Many women cringe at the idea of being intimate with other women. They say, *"I'm never eating pussy!"* or *"I would never let a girl go down on me!"* First and foremost, never say never. I thought I was "strictly dickly" until I tasted my friend's pussy. That said, would you be surprised if I told you that not every woman in the Lifestyle likes to be intimate with women? Some LS women aren't sexually attracted to other women and may only engage in sex with them to solely please their men. Others don't engage in any sort of sexual activity with women at all and will make that very clear when approached. From my experience, only about 60% of LS women truly desire to please other women sexually. Twenty-five percent of them are still trying to figure out what they want and who they are in the Lifestyle, while the remaining 15% aren't interested in women at all.

Let me make this clear; a woman does not have to be bisexual to be in the Lifestyle. Nor does she have to want women sexually in order to be in a non-monogamous relationship with a man. At the most fundamental level, a woman should have an understanding of what she needs sexually and emotionally and be open to the endless possibilities that exist to have her needs fulfilled by both women and men. She must also be open to allowing her partner to have his needs fulfilled in whatever manner is pleasing to him, which more than likely will include other women. To be comfortable in this space, she must be ready and willing to embrace her own sexuality so that potential opportunities for growth aren't blocked.

Initially, it may not be easy for a woman to embrace her sexuality especially if she was raised to believe that sexual relations should only happen between one man and one woman. However, the reality is that a woman's sexuality can vary from straight to bi to downright freak and accepting that variation within herself is key to unlocking the door that blocks her from emotional and sexual freedom.

A woman in the Lifestyle who owns her sexuality is a gift to the entire community. She is confident and comfortable in her body and is able to articulate what she enjoys, while also tending to the needs of her partners. She doesn't have to be one thing. She can be all things if that is what she chooses and no one has the right to dictate how or from whom she derives fulfillment from.

There are typically five different types of women you'll interact with in the LS environment; straight, bi-friendly, bi-curious, bi-sexual, and lesbian. Every woman needs to understand which one she most identifies with and if she's anything other than straight, she must figure out the type of woman she's interested in. Here's a quick breakdown of the types of women I've interacted with since my Lifestyle journey began.

* **Straight**: This woman is not interested in women at all. She has no desire to flirt with women or have them flirt with her. She's on the Lifestyle scene because she cares about her man's happiness and wants him to have his sexual needs met by other women. During sex play, she may watch her man fuck another woman while she plays with her pussy, or she may participate by fucking on her man while he pleases the other woman. She'll cheer him on and suck his dick to keep him erect so he can perform well. She and the other woman have a clear understanding that both

of them are there for his pleasure only, and he, in turn, will please them both.

A straight woman in the Lifestyle is a real rider. This woman is content with the man in her life but understands that he desires to have his needs fulfilled by other women. She cares about his happiness, and because she wants to be with him, she consents to his other sexual or emotional relationships. A lot of the women that are in polygamous relationships are straight women who have consented to this type of Lifestyle.

* **Bi-curious**: This woman likes to flirt with and tease other women, but she is not with the shits. She will play nice, she may touch a woman while laughing at a joke, and maybe let a woman touch her in a friendly way, but she's not with pussy action. She's absolutely free with compliments *"Oh, you're really pretty,"* or *"Damn, girl, your body is fire. Can I touch your ass?"*, or my all-time fave, *"If I liked girls, I would fuck you."* Initially, a bi-sexual freak like me thinks, *"Oh, she might be into me."* But the more I'm around these types, the more I realize that women just love to flirt. Sometimes it's hard to differentiate between the "just being flirty" types from the "I lick pussy and love it" types. This could land you in a bit of trouble because if you're more aggressive and go in for a full hug with some ass grabbing, the Bi-curious girl will quickly maneuver away from you and give a look like, "that's too much". She may blush and give a little smile, but she'll quickly walk away, regretting she ever stopped you.

I can't lie; the Bi-curious types are hella confusing! Maybe it's because I'm a woman and I know that when I flirt with someone, it's usually because I'm attracted to them. When I have no interest in a person, man or woman, I make it as clear as possible that I'm not interested. So when a woman flirts with me, especially in the LS environment, I tend to assume that it's sexual. In Vanilla spaces, I already know there's a 50/50 chance that the girl is just flirting, so I chill and wait to see how far the flirting goes. I generally feel like the women in LS spaces are more likely to be interested in other women. However, the Bi-curious types make finding women playmates way more challenging because their behavior is so confusing.

* **Bi-friendly**: This woman is attracted to other women, but she usually just tests the waters. She will kiss a woman in the mouth to see what that feels like. If it's pleasing, she'll do it again. If she finds an attraction to a woman, she may let that woman kiss her breasts or even play with her pussy at a particular time without anyone else knowing. Eventually, when she gets more comfortable with her attraction to women, she'll let women play with her more. She may even try licking a pussy or two, but she's not aggressive about it. She won't go out hunting for pussy, but if some pussy comes her way, she'll play around with the idea of having it. She'll also enjoy women from time to time with her man because she knows that's what he likes, but she usually needs some directing from him to do so.

Disappointingly enough, I've had my fair share of the Bi-friendly lady. No judgment really, if this is your thing. It's just frustrating as hell. She will give you all the vibes and have you thinking you have a real chance to have her, but will eventually shut shit down. There was a woman I desired so much that initially, I didn't recognize that she wasn't really into women when I had sex with her and her husband. Eventually, I became less interested in fucking them because her sex energy was too low for me. Over the years, we became really good friends, having sex periodically, and then she came clean one day. *"I hope you don't get offended by me saying this. I don't want to have a sexual relationship with you anymore. I really like you and enjoy your company, but I would prefer just to be friends. I'm not really into women like that, and I just told my husband, if I don't want to lick a woman's pussy then I'm not going to. I've been doing it for him, but now I don't want to do things I don't want to do."*

Respectfully, I get it, but sheesh! Bi-friendly women are hard fucking work! They do, then they don't, sometimes it's difficult to keep track. The only thing to do is pull back and respect what she is willing to do at that time, and when she's ready for sexual contact, she will let you know. If you happen to fall into the Bi-friendly category, the best things you can do for everyone involved is move at your own pace, don't allow anyone to pressure you into doing things you don't want to do, and just be true to yourself.

* **Bi-sexual**: This woman enjoys having sex with both men and women. *Did you feel the smile in my words as you read them?* This does not necessarily mean equally. It just means she finds pleasure in sexual encounters with both genders. She enjoys getting fucked by a man while sucking on sweet pussy, and she can be alone with a man or woman and manage to find what she needs to please her. She can also have both at the same time and feel ultimate pleasure. In LS environments, she is the easiest type to find pleasure with because she's sure of what she likes, and she isn't afraid to get it. If she's with her man, she will help him find women both of them can enjoy for the moment or a lifetime.

Bi-sexual women are obviously highly favored in the Lifestyle, whether she is a Unicorn or in a relationship. She's typically sure of what she desires and seeks compatible playmates for her and her man. Couples seeking single women or other couples more often prefer women who are bi-sexual so that they can be playmates for both partners, but again it isn't required. I don't like to label myself because I'm somewhat of a savage, but bi-sexual would be the closest type to my sexual identity. As a bi-scxual woman, I have strong desires for both men and women, although my preference is men. There is something about a woman; her softness, her weakness, her breasts, her hair, her hips that swallow her waist, that makes her absolutely fascinating to me. Albeit not from the first try, the taste of a woman is the sweetest taste I can imagine, and when it's fresh and wet, all I want to do is devour it. Yet, I am not complete in that moment. I can't feel whole until the strength of a man is present. There is something about a strong, virile man fucking me that is intoxicating, and being with a woman can't match that.

* **Lesbian**: This is a woman who isn't a man and is attracted to non-men. Apparently, there are more than twenty different types of lesbians which are far too many to go into detail in this book. To keep it brief and so as not to offend any of my lesbian readers, I am going to merely differentiate lesbian types solely on outward appearance. A lesbian can be the lipstick or femme type, defined as women who are feminine-looking in appearance and behavior. Or she can be a stud or butch, defined as women who have more of a masculine appearance. These descriptions are not meant to be offensive, stereotypical, or place anyone in a box. I respect the variations of Les types and realize there's much more involved than merely "a look". That said, lesbians who enjoy the energy and the openness of the Lifestyle environment will attend events seeking potential partners or playmates. They enjoy a good time and realize there is a large pool of women willing to play with other women in those spaces. Some of them will also entertain men if that's what they desire at that time. If you happen to approach a lesbian, do not assume she is unwilling to play with a couple or with a single man. In those environments, people typically step outside of their comfort zones to try new things. Never make

assumptions about anyone because you could miss out on many great experiences.

When I originally wrote this part in "Let Me Fuck Your Husband", I thought about lesbians in a completely different way. Recently, while at an LS party, I assumed that because two women were together they wouldn't be interested in having sex with me and my male partner. However, one of the females approached me and asked if we would be interested in playing with her and her partner. To my surprise, not only did I enjoy both of them, but my friend also had the pleasure of fucking them as well. Of course, he was beside himself thinking he busted a couple of cherries that night. But the only thing that really got busted was his nut and his ego when he found out he was absolutely not the first man they had sex with.

After our sexual encounter, all of us chatted about stereotypes, particularly as they pertained to lesbians and I realized that I too had certain misconceptions about them. The most important truth I learned was that all lesbians don't run from dick. Ha! I knew then that when I began the revisions for this book, changing the lesbian portion was imperative. For someone as open as I am, I wrote some real close-minded shit the first time. But don't hold it against me, I am also a work in progress.

In any case, the type of woman you choose to engage with is a personal choice based on your preferences, your needs, and the agreements you've made with your partner. As you have more encounters with the many varieties of women, you will get a feel for which types work better for the both of you.

Please understand that a woman does not have to be "bi" anything to be in the Lifestyle. If you're a woman and the mere thought of being intimate with another woman makes your skin crawl, that's okay. Women are simply not for you. But don't let the lack of the desire to eat pussy dissuade your choice to be non-monogamous. That said, your feelings shouldn't negate the fact that your man is interested in other women and will want your consent to have them. Having consideration for your partner's happiness is what the Lifestyle is all about. Once a woman establishes the level of interest she has in women, she and her partner can then determine the kind of non-monogamous relationship they will have and create a formula that will make both of them happy.

There are many different types of relationships in the Lifestyle. Some are more complex than others. There are couples who only seek partners that are interested in long-term relationships, while others are strictly looking for sex without any emotional connections. Keep in mind that you and your partner may desire different things, so you need to have open and honest conversations about what you truly want. Maybe your man always fantasized about being in a relationship with someone who also likes to have sex with other women. He may fantasize about having sex with multiple women along with you, or he could desire to be alone with different women in more intimate settings. Perhaps your woman fantasizes about getting DP'd with you and a friend from work or maybe she just wants a man to fuck her good without having to do anything for him in return. Each of you fantasizes about something and although they may not be the same things, they should be discussed openly and freely. No matter the specifics, if you never have the conversations, how will you ever know what your partner truly desires? The belief that you should look to your partner to provide all things is unrealistic, and you know that because you've experienced it. Monogamy may be for some, but it's definitely not for everyone. Consensual non-monogamous relationships are transcendent with a magic of their own. They are divinely liberating allowing space for one to free oneself from the misconception that you can only find happiness in one person. You and your partner only need to determine your needs and decide which type works best for you.

NON-MONOGAMY IN THE BLACK

"Black couples shy away from single men as it is less common for Black men to want other men to fuck their wives."

My first non-monogamous relationship was an open one. I'll admit I was a little unsure about it at first, maybe even a little afraid. I was dating a man that I was growing to love, but we had never really been truly honest with who we were and what we wanted. We both knew and admitted that monogamy was foolery, and we didn't want any parts of it.

Now what that looked like for me, I wasn't quite sure of, and neither was he. But he did have a basic understanding of what he would need before *embarking on any relationship. As we got closer and our connection became more serious, he was very forthcoming with his specific requirements. His main stipulation before getting serious with any woman was that she would have to fuck other men. This is not a normal prerequisite for a relationship, so you can understand why I was caught off guard. He told me that he could not be with a one-man woman because he was not a one-woman man. He knew this about himself far longer than I realized the same about me. Neither of us had experience in non-monogamous relationships, so we were traversing new territory. Our chemistry was mind-blowing. We connected on so many levels; conversing was easy, we belly laughed together and our sex energy was unmatched. He was very well endowed and his sex drive paralleled mine.* Those that actually know me know that I like to fuck and often. There have been very few men capable of satisfying my insatiable appetite for sex. He was one of those men. Yet here he was telling me he wanted me to fuck other men.

When we first started dating, he and I lived in different states, so we would only get together on the weekends. During this time, I was still seeing and fucking several other men during the week. I did not make this known to him. When he initially wanted to discuss the possibility of a relationship, he scared me off because I still didn't know how to tell him that I wanted other men. I was only divorced two years at that time, so I was not ready for any kind of relationship. I was also not comfortable saying, "We're great together, but I'm interested in other dick too". Instead, I blew him off.

We stopped dealing with each other for a while. But two years later, while working in DC, we rekindled our connection. By this time, I was honest in my intentions to be free of monogamous norms, but I had not yet vocalized my true desires to him. He knew that I was attracted to women, but I didn't want him to know how much I also enjoyed fucking a variety of men. It wasn't an easy conversation for me to have, considering I wasn't sure how comfortable I would be with him knowing that about me. Subsequently, I also avoided talking to him about what he desired or enjoyed. On the other hand, he wanted to be more expressive with me and share the sexual experiences he had with other women. I remember him telling me about a girl he fucked while I was away. He told me the details about how they met up, he liked her, and then he took her home and fucked the shit out of her. The details surprisingly turned me on, but I felt guilty about his openness. I wasn't ready to reveal myself as he had. I knew that if he had asked me about my weekend in Vegas, I probably wouldn't have been as honest with him about the man I fucked.

Things can be funny that way. Here it was, I'd entered into the world of non-monogamy, I made a choice to be free with my sexuality, yet, I was still afraid of being judged. I soon realized that I was uncomfortable with showing myself to him. I was afraid he would ultimately like me less if he knew I enjoyed sex with others. It's not an easy concept to digest initially; that someone you cared about could understand that your feelings toward him had little to do with the sexual desires that needed to be fulfilled by others.

Once I set my fears aside, we finally had the conversation about our real desires. I felt like a huge weight was lifted from me and he was actually relieved that I needed what I needed, because he was free to be his true self. We began to discuss the details of our sexual encounters with others with such ease that eventually, it became our thing. We bonded more when we discussed our experiences, how the sex felt, or how good or bad of a lay a person was. Often, the conversation would lead to a late-night trip to the other's bed because we were so turned on by the explicit details of the other's night with someone else. The details, in essence, helped us to feel safe, which is important when you're sharing your partner with others.

As we moved forward in the relationship, we discussed what we needed most. We both needed the existence of the opportunity to have sex with other *people. We didn't want to fuck other people all of the time, but knowing the opportunity was there to utilize when needed, was everything.*

Some of you may be thinking "what in the entire fuck?" But yes, this was how our open relationship began. We were two individuals who were ready to step away from the norm and do what felt good in our hearts, not what society said we should do. We wanted to have a relationship that was open and freeing so we figured out to do that. I never thought I could enjoy hearing or watching someone I loved find pleasure in other women. Yet sharing him and being shared was the thing that I began to desire the most within our relationship. It may be hard for you to imagine that sharing your partner could be a pleasurable experience. This is especially true if you started your relationship with a monogamous foundation. Transforming your relationship into something that looks very different from how you began will be difficult initially, but it is possible if it's what you truly desire.

As discussed earlier, the first place to start is changing how you think about sex and love. If you can't learn to differentiate and separate the two, you will never be able to share the joy your partner feels when he/she is having sex with other people, nor will you be able to have sex with others and not confuse the good feelings with love. This may seem like an impossible feat for my married readers. You may be thinking that this kind of behavior is for people who don't believe in the sanctity of marriage. But you're wrong. I have friends who were married for over ten years before changing what their relationship looked like. Some have serious long-term lovers, and others have casual sex at parties just for fun. There are many different ways to fashion your relationship and many things you can choose to do differently from others. Everything ain't for everybody. It's a fact that rings true, especially in the Lifestyle. You and your partner will determine what's right for you but first, you must understand the types of non-monogamous relationships that exist.

In this next part of the book, I am going to describe the basic structures of non-monogamous relationships. I also decided to provide you with the prevalence of these relationships within Black culture due to the underrepresentation of Black folks in the Lifestyle. Considering many of us think only White people are non-monogamous, it was important for me to give people of color an honest look at how prevalent these relationships are within the LS community.

* **Polyamory** (meaning multiple loves): In this form of a relationship, the partners involved give consent to having multiple sexual and/or loving relationships with others. There are many different forms of polyamorous relationships and many ways the people involved choose to formulate their specific relationship. Here's a quick breakdown of several types:

  ◦ **Mono-poly:** where one partner identifies as monogamous but the other identifies as polyamorous

  ◦ **Solo-poly:** a person considers himself/herself their own primary partner and prioritizes their own needs with no obligation to their partners

  ◦ **Hierarchical-poly:** where some relationships have more authority or importance than the others (primary, secondary, tertiary, etc.)

  ◦ **Non hierarchical-poly:** no relationship is prioritized over the others. Each relationship is unique and decisions are made based on what works for the group

  ◦ **Vee:** where one person has relationships with two people who are not involved with one another

  ◦ **Triad or throuple:** where all three partners are sexually and romantically involved with one another

○ **Quad:** relationship between four people who are sexually and romantically involved in a variety of ways

The list can go on depending on the number of partners involved and the level of involvement they have between each other. Polyamory is similar to the other forms of CNM relationships with sex being allowed with other partners. The main difference between polyamory and let's say swingers or open relationships is that there tends to be less reluctance to hinder romantic or emotional connections between lovers.

Prevalence in Black Couples: From my experience, polyamory seems to be the most common relationship type among Black Lifestyle couples; with the triad type in combination with a hierarchical component being predominant. Typically, Black polyamorous couples will have one or more girlfriends. Rarely will the relationship include other males or boyfriends. Even more rare is the male bi-sexual. The two partners typically seek out women to form a triad but agree that the primary relationship is the two of them and will be the relationship with the highest priority. The primaries may cohabitate, have children, develop business relationships and combine finances with one another, but rarely are subsequent relationships that involved. The primaries dictate how they can explore any secondary relationships and they usually have "veto" power which allows either of them to end any of the other relationships if things become problematic.

Pros: Polyamory provides the opportunity for increased romantic and sexual gratification from other partners. When the primary female partner is bi-sexual, but connections with other men are not wanted or allowed, she gets her needs met by the girlfriend(s) and her husband. When the primaries find female partners that both enjoy spending time with, they get the added benefit of sharing the partner together.

Cons: It is rare to see Black polyamorous units that include more than one man. If polyamory is supposed to be about loving and connecting more freely with multiple partners, where is the regard for women who desire to have multiple male partners? Polyandry which is the practice of a woman having more than one "husband" is frowned upon even by other polyamorists. I have yet to encounter Black quad units that include two couples, each consisting of one man and a woman that have varying sexual or romantic relationships among them. Even in a world where having multiple partners is accepted, it's only truly acceptable if it applies to a man. This is most likely due to the fact that Black men are less likely to share women they love with other men. They are more likely to share a female lover/friend or a friend with benefits with other men, but not someone they love or have emotional attachments to. Because of this, the primary female partner rarely has her sexual needs met by other men. This can sometimes lead the woman to stray to find the emotional or sexual connection she desires elsewhere.

* **Polygamy** (meaning a man having more than one wife): In this form of relationship, a man is "married" to more than one wife. The wives are typically not sexually involved with one another and are considered co-wives or sister-wives. Ideally, the husband loves all of the women equally, fathers children by them, and may choose to live in a communal home, or have separate homes, for each wife and family. If you watched "Big Love", a series on HBO, the main family were polygamists. Each wife had her own house, gave birth to children fathered by the same man, and worked together as a family unit to accomplish common

goals. Polygamy is typically seen in religious communities such as the Muslims or Mormons, but it is illegal in the United States and is punishable by fine, imprisonment, or both. However, when polygamy is practiced in the U.S., the husband is usually legally married to one wife and the subsequent female partners may be referred to as "wives" without any legal responsibilities or commitments.

Prevalence in Black Couples: Regardless of the legal ramifications, polygamy is practiced in Black relationships. Although not the most common form of relationships among Black Lifestyle couples, polygamy is generally accepted in Black Muslim communities and amongst those that believe that polygamy is more advantageous to the longevity of Black love and the Black family. Polygamy is not supposed to be about satisfying the man's need for more sex; however, he does have that as an additional benefit.

Historically, the purpose of multiple wives was to ensure that widows and fatherless children had a caregiver after the husbands died during wartime. Obviously, that is not a common issue in modern times, although the high rate of Black men who are incarcerated in the U.S. prison system has led to a lack of available and suitable Black men to marry wives and father children. Modern-day Black polygamists contend that polygamy these days has more to do with saving the Black family and ensuring more Black women and children have fathers and husbands in their lives. They also choose polygamy to build larger families and have shared businesses and wealth. Although his financial burden is greater, if childbearing is involved, he is able to have other children if the family wishes to have more children or if a wife isn't able to do so.

Pros: The burden of having to please the husband is shared between the wives. Some women merely lack the desire to be consistently intimate with one man or she may be too busy with her career, education, or other family obligations to keep her husband fulfilled. Having another "wife", relieves her of the burden of being solely responsible to maintain his happiness. Within polygamy, the husband benefits from having additional loving relationships and may have a decreased desire to look for sex and love outside of the relationship. The children also have the benefit of having multiple mothers to raise and nurture them. If the husband and wife choose wisely and pick a sister wife with her own income stream, they may have the increased benefit of having multiple incomes towards the household.

Cons: The "wives" are typically forbidden from engaging in any sort of relationship with men whom they have no relation to. This means that two or more sister wives share their love, time, and affection for one man, who may or may not be capable of fulfilling the needs of all wives equally. Polygamists love to say that it isn't about sex, "it's about community." Although sex may not be the primary reason for the polygamist union, sex does play a huge role in those relationships. In polygamy it is expected for women to deal with the hand they are dealt. If a wife is unfulfilled or treated poorly by her husband, there is little she can do with the exception of divorce, and that's only if it is permitted. When a sexually ill-equipped man is responsible for satisfying the sexual desires of all the wives, this limits the amount of attention and sexual gratification either of them receives. What's worse, if the man is a mediocre lay, the wives will live the remainder of their lives with unfulfilled desires and lame dick. However, when a man is unfulfilled or unhappy with his wife, or if he simply wants more, he can go out to find others to satisfy his needs. In my opinion, polygamy is very one-sided when it comes to the fulfillment of a woman's needs. Okay sure the husband may be paying the bills, but that shouldn't negate the fact that women have desires and deserve to be sexually and emotionally fulfilled.

* **Swingers:** These relationships consist of partners who have agreed to sex with other people usually within certain settings. Typically emotional and romantic attachments are not being formed between new partners which makes these relationships less complicated and a lot more fun. Couples that swing can be married or unmarried and participate in sex with single men, women, or other couples, who themselves may or may not be married. Couples can be full swap, meaning penetrative sex is allowed with other partners, or soft swap, meaning partners may be able to have oral sex, but penetration is not allowed. Many married couples who swing, and are full swap, prefer to have sex with other married couples. Married couples feel safer when they know that everyone involved would be compromising their own relationship if things go awry. However, most couples, regardless of marital status, tend to seek both Unicorns and/or Bulls to fulfill their needs.

A Unicorn, especially a beautiful one, is a gem, and a Lifestyle favorite. A Unicorn is bisexual, single, free, and can engage in sex with whomever she pleases; all she has to do is say yes. Couples who seek out Unicorns desire unforgettable sexual experiences that are fulfilling for both partners. When dealing with a Unicorn, the couple understands that she is there for a good time, not a long time. However, some Unicorns may be interested in longer-term arrangements that could include completing a triad or another form of a non-monogamous relationship.

On the other hand, single men or Bulls, are not as highly favored amongst non-full swap couples. A Bull on the Lifestyle scene runs the risk of being viewed as a pariah if he doesn't make friends quickly with either a Unicorn or a friendly husband. Very few husbands want single men lurking around their naked wives without pussy of their own to offer. Yet, Bulls are often approached by some of these married or coupled men and propositioned to fuck their female partners. Although it is more common for White couples to specifically seek Black Bulls to fuck their wives, Bull hunting does occur within the Black demographic of the Lifestyle community. However, it isn't always easy to find willing Bulls to fulfill this need because most LS events don't allow single men to attend. This is done to keep the amount of single males to a minimum. Otherwise, there would be single men arriving in pacts, expecting to fuck anything moving, with zero respect for people's relationships or LS etiquette.

Now, swinger couples who are unmarried or not in committed relationships may not share the same disdain for Bulls. Unmarried swinger couples typically include long-time lovers, or friends with benefits, that get together to "swing." When there is a healthy quantity of available Bulls, Unicorns have the pick of the litter and may snatch one up and agree to operate together to full swap with other couples for the night. Some full swap couples may turn down a Unicorn if she doesn't have dick of her own to offer, especially if the female in the relationship isn't Bi, and would prefer to have sex with a man. When a Unicorn and a Bull form a pact and present themselves as a couple or a duo, they have the benefit of offering the partner as an equal trade to another couple. This is not a deceitful tactic, as long as both parties are honest in revealing the context of the relationship when asked. The non-committed swinger couple may turn off some married couples, but generally, if the friends are attractive and meet the criteria for a hookup, the married or committed couple will most likely be willing to fuck.

Prevalence in Black Couples: Swinging may not be the most common relationship style among Black married and unmarried Lifestylers but it is a more common behavior. A couple can be polyamorous or polygamous and still be swingers. I like to think of swinging more as behavior than a specific type of relationship. I once believed that Black married couples who swung were mostly interested in soft swap interactions. But as I continued my Lifestyle journey and immersed myself more into the swinging communities, I realized that many Black couples full swap, but they generally do so in the privacy of their own homes. I was once a sex and swinger convention type of woman. I thought that if I went to the places that brought larger crowds, I would increase my chances of finding the kind of playmates I was searching for. I later discovered that I was wrong. Since writing the original version of this portion of the book in 2021, I have been to more than twenty-five swinger parties that were either in someone's home or at a location disclosed only to invited people. More than a few of those were orchestrated by yours truly. Black people love to swing! They just don't go around telling people what they do in order to avoid scrutiny and judgment.

Pros: If it's a full swap couple, either married or unmarried, both partners can have their desires fulfilled from both men and women of other couples or singles. Assuming neither of the males are interested in male-to-male contact, as Bi-sexual contact in Black swinging couples isn't common, all parties can find fulfillment from their partners of choice. The wife also gets the benefit of receiving pleasure from a woman and another man. The men should set clear boundaries on male-to-male contact prior to sexual contact when necessary.

Cons: Wives of soft swap couples cannot be sexually fulfilled through penetration by any other man, even if that is what she desires. If she is Bi-sexual, she can have her needs fulfilled by women, but she must be content with the dick her husband is serving her. Soft swap couples have limited opportunities with full swap couples due to the unavailability of penetrative sex with the soft swap wife. Sometimes the wives will play alone or while the husbands watch, but ultimately the full swap husband wants to fuck and will find pussy elsewhere. Couples can lose track of each other in the relationship if the focus is predominantly on the swinging and not each other. Finding time to be alone with each other is essential. Swinger relationships can get messy if the parties involved aren't clear about another couple's specific needs and boundaries. If a couple swings with another couple regularly, it is possible that one of the playmates develops feelings for a partner of the other couple. These things can happen but should be openly discussed to prevent resentment or the collapse of either relationship.

Here is where I will address the stigma around multiple sex partners and sexually transmitted infections (STIs). A common reason that gives pause to many who may consider swinging is the perceived increased risk for STIs. Although the risk is bothersome for many on the fence about swinging, research suggests that the risk of transmitting STIs is no higher than they are among monogamous people.[6] What people fail to realize is that non-monogamous people tend to get tested more often and are more open about their results than are monogamous individuals, who pretend to have one sex partner but are really engaging in sex with others outside of the relationship without their partner's knowledge. Ultimately, there are more non-monogamous people who are aware of their conditions and getting treatments when necessary, and fewer people unknowingly transmitting infections. There is no way to guarantee any person is disease-free 100% of the time unless you get tested together and remain attached at the hip at all times, which is silly and unrealistic. Even then, it only takes one trip to the bathroom stall to suck and fuck a willing food server when you're supposed to be taking a shit. Most so-called monogamous people typically ask a potential partner if they're "clean" or not, then move into action with nothing more than the person's word. From my experience, men who are married or in relationships are the main culprits desiring unprotected sex. Because they fuck their partners raw, they tend to struggle with condom use and either can't get hard or stay hard when forced to use one. I use the word "forced" because believe it or not, "monogamous" men are in these streets reckless as fuck, trying to run up in any pretty little thing, raw. Whether you accept it or not, in group sex situations, with true Lifestylers, condoms are plentiful and are used regularly and effectively. However, if multiple partners agree to fluid bonding (unprotected sex), recent test results and/or new STI testing are typically required.

No sex is 100% safe whether you are monogamous or non-monogamous. The most important advice I can give is to practice safe sex and get tested at least bi-annually or quarterly to ease your mind. There is no shortage of condoms which come in a variety of sizes, textures, and flavors. If you are going to have sex with multiple partners, wrap your fucking dick up! If you're concerned with catching an STI through oral sex or kissing, then use barriers to prevent transmission or simply don't suck dick or lick pussy. On a personal level, I get tested at least every six months and keep an electronic copy of my results to provide when asked. That helps to ease a partner's mind in the moment because they know that at a minimum, I am aware that STIs are real and that I may not be reckless out here in these streets. Be smart and wrap it up to protect yourself and others.

* **Open**: This relationship style is probably the most freeing type of all non-monogamous relationships. They can get tricky, so they must be treated with great care and accountability. Similar to that of swingers, open relationships have different levels, but they can be less complicated as long as boundaries are set and respected. In open relationships, both husband and wife are free to have sex with whomever they please within the limitations set by the couple. They choose their own playmates, who may or may not be introduced to the other partner. But if they enjoy sharing one another with others together, they may decide to set aside time to have threesomes, moresomes, or attend LS events where they have increased opportunities for sharing to occur. Either of the partners may have the option to have sexual and/or emotional relationships with their playmates. It all depends on the agreements made between the primary couple. Boundary setting and honest communication are essential in any relationship but are crucial in open relationships for the primary relationship to survive the openness. Both partners create clear boundaries that help one another feel safe, secure, and loved. One must know that any boundary can be changed or amended as long as both partners have agreed. Time and space should be dedicated for both partners to check-in, express feelings of hurt or insecurity, and provide reassurance when needed.

Open relationships are not for the faint at heart. They work better with individuals who are great at keeping the emotion out of sex.

Typically, loving relationships are not being formed outside of the primary relationship but can happen if the couple agrees to them. Although open relationships can be somewhat easier to navigate, due to both partners' ability to limit emotional attachments, if the primary relationship isn't strong and the trust isn't irrefutable, the relationship will not make it through problems that will inevitably arise.

Prevalence in Black Couples: Open relationships are not common in Black couples or the Lifestyle community at large. It is more challenging to get through feelings of jealousy and insecurity when you are consistently not present during the sexual encounters your partner has. It is also easier to feel neglected when your partner has regular playdates that do not include you. My first non-monogamous relationship was open, and it took years before meeting other Black couples who were completely open. It is not an easy relationship to be a part of, however, if the two people involved are committed to making it work, it is possible to have a successful open relationship.

Pros: Both partners have the opportunity to be sexually and emotionally fulfilled by the people they choose. When the approval of a playmate or lover isn't required, either can choose individuals that meet their specific needs. If one partner searches for playmates in different spaces than the other, it's possible for them to bring multiple like-minded individuals together, who may not have met otherwise, and create a highly fuckable Lifestyle community. Often, when partners seek sex in the same space, it's harder to find couples who are a total package that can meet the needs of both partners.

Cons: There are fewer opportunities for partner sharing together because chances are, the chosen outside lovers are not in the

Lifestyle and may not be interested in group sex of any kind. Therefore, extramarital sex occurs more often without the presence of the other partner. That said, if either member of the primary couple is insecure, an open relationship would never work. There will be times when either partner may feel insecure, but every hookup should not lead to a therapy session about his or her insecurities. The communication between the primary partners must also be remarkable, or else the primary relationship will fail. Both partners must trust the other completely because doubt is a seed that will grow a life of its own once planted. I must point out that there is ample opportunity for others to infiltrate the primary relationship and possibly "steal" one of the partners away if either of them isn't firmly adhering to boundaries to prevent that from happening. For this reason, it is a must that both partners ensure their lovers also respect and comply with the boundaries set forth by the primary partners.

Whether you're interested in loving multiple people or just fucking them, you can tailor your relationship to whatever makes you and your partner happy. There's no wrong or right way to Lifestyle, and that's one of the best things about it. How and why you choose non-monogamy is your business and does not need to be explained to anyone. No relationship begins the same way and every person that chooses the Lifestyle does so for different reasons.

It is common for people to believe that women are somehow coerced into non-monogamous relationships because *"why would a woman willingly share her man?"* Yes, it is true that men are more likely to initiate the idea. However, most women choose non-monogamy because it is more conducive to their overall happiness and security in their relationships. Obviously, every woman doesn't begin her Lifestyle journey at the same place in life. Some women choose non-monogamy after being repeatedly hurt by men they fall in love with. Others fall in love and choose non-mo-nogamy to keep their man sexually satisfied, while others decide they want to be non-monogamous because they are sexually free and want to have certain fantasies fulfilled by people outside of their relationship. The choice to become non-monogamous is a decision that should be made with a clear heart and mind, not under pressure or duress. If you feel pres-sured by a partner, ask for space and take the time you need to make an informed decision. Although avoiding pain is never a good reason to enter into non-monogamy, understanding that you can minimize the pain that occurs from typical broken monogamous relationships may be the deter-mining factor that sways you to give the Lifestyle a try.

Nina & Darius met in 2009. Both had previously been in long-term monogamous relationships with other people. He was divorced, and she'd recently broken up with her boyfriend. Darius no longer wanted to be in monogamous relationships. He was tired of the cheating and lying he did in his first marriage, so he decided to be honest with women he dated about his need for variety. After about a month of dating, Darius felt like Nina could be the one. Nina was falling hard for him, so he decided to pull the trigger. He told himself, "it was now or never." Although he knew there was a chance she wouldn't go for it, he was willing to lose what he wanted to get what he needed.

One evening, as they talked over dinner, he told her how much he loved her, that he could see a future with her, and then he bluntly said, *"But I'm going to need new pussy now and then."* Nina was thrown off and didn't understand what he was saying. She was falling in love with him and believed he felt the same. She was hurt, *"I broke down in tears and asked him why I wasn't enough for him."* He explained how he cheated in his past relationships, and he no longer wanted to live that way. He needed her to understand that if they were going to be together, she would have to accept that he couldn't fuck one person for the rest of his life. It was an unrealistic expectation for him, and he was tired of hurting the women he loved. He reassured her that the sex he had with others would not change how he felt about her. He explained, *"I can just fuck and be out. It has nothing to do with emotion. But I know me, and I have to have other pussy."* Nina admitted that hearing him say those words made her feel insecure. But what was the alternative? *"I went along with it because I loved him and didn't want to lose him."* She also expressed her appreciation for his honesty and respected him for not wanting to be like the men she used to date, *"I never had a man tell me straight up that he needed to fuck other women to be happy."*

As she contemplated what Darius had thrown at her, she had one major concern. Where would she be when he had sex with other women? Darius told her that, ideally, she would be present and participating. Nina wasn't sure what that would be like for her. She had never been intimate with a woman at all. She found some women attractive or sexy, but she hadn't even kissed a girl before, and now she was expected to have sex with them? It was a lot, but she knew it would make him happy and was willing to give it a try.

The first time they had a threesome, she admitted feeling nervous about how she thought she would feel watching the man she loved fuck someone else, but instead felt something completely different. She admits, *"Shockingly, I was turned on. It was weird. I didn't feel jealous at all. I saw how happy he was and how much he enjoyed having both of us at the same time. The sex between him and I got much better after that."*

She didn't touch the other woman at all the first time. They were at a Lifestyle club, and she wasn't comfortable yet in that environment. But, eventually, she became more comfortable with interacting with women. She disclosed how she interacts with women, *"I'm not that aggressive with the women we have sex with. He usually directs me when he wants to see me interact more. But, when we find someone I really like, someone that's really sexy with good energy, I enjoy doing more."*

Nina & Darius have been married four years and are very happy together. They are currently looking for a girlfriend in hopes of creating their own closed triad unit. They don't like swinging. Nina doesn't want to have sex with other men, and Darius isn't too thrilled about the idea either. Both agree that if she changes her mind, they will revisit the topic at that time. For now, they like the idea of having a serious relationship with a woman they both really like; however, Nina has some reservations.

"I had concerns as we started looking for another woman for us. Fucking is one thing, but the possibility of him loving another woman, I wasn't so sure about that. We found someone we like, and I can already tell she's getting attached to him. What if she starts to love him?"

Nina realized that dealing with her emotions about Darius sharing his love with another woman was harder than dealing with the sex. But, if they want to get serious with the other woman, she also knows that she has to be open to the reality of that happening. *"The other woman deserves to be loved too. It's not fair for me to say that I want us to have a serious relationship with a woman but then place regulations on how it happens. I'm just not prepared for him to love somebody else."*

Darius acknowledges that it's his responsibility to control his emotions and balance the flow of his emotions between the two women. He doesn't want Nina to think he would love her less if his feelings blossomed for the other. He affirmed, *"Each relationship has to be watered. Nina is my queen and will always be. I will reassure her of that as often as I need to. However, the two of them should also develop their own relationship. Once they care about each other, it will most likely soften the blow."* ~ Nina & Darius est. 2009

Nina's entryway into the Lifestyle is not unlike what many women experience. Some women are initially introduced to the Lifestyle by the men they're dating. These women are fortunate because most men are not brave enough to honestly express their thirst for other women. They'd rather conduct completely separate lives rather than tell a woman, "I need other pussy." Nina was hurt initially, but, after careful consideration, decided that she didn't want to lose the man she loved because he wanted to enjoy sex with other women. In Nina's situation, it was her man that initiated the idea of sexual freedom and his desire to be in a non-monogamous relationship. However, some women also introduce and draw their partners into the Lifestyle. The choice to be in a non-monogamous relationship doesn't have to be out of fear of losing a partner or keeping the peace. Women also want to enjoy sexual freedom, and it is those women who present the opportunity for "more" to their men.

Gina and Martin met in 2002 and married a year later. During their first thirteen years of marriage, both of them had been guilty of infidelity, but they managed to keep the marriage intact. Gina began to realize that she had certain desires that weren't being fulfilled in her relationship. When she watched porn, she loved to watch the women pleasing each other. Although she had never been intimate with a woman before (her only girl experience was when she was young and dry humped her neighbor), she found her curiosity about touching a woman peaking. She would get turned on from watching two women scissoring each other or strapping on to fuck one another. Gina expressed clearly, *"I wanted to experience what it felt like being with a woman, and I knew I would be turned on watching Martin please other women."*

She began researching how to go about getting what she desired and discovered swinging. She presented the idea to Martin, who was not easily swayed. He knew that Gina really liked dick and wasn't sure if this was a gateway for getting what *she* really wanted. But, he did like the idea of having permission to fuck other women, as it was something he wanted to do anyway. He eventually agreed to a non-monogamous relationship as long as they found women interested in fucking both of them.

One night, they decided to go to one of the sex clubs Gina looked into. She and Martin were having a good time mixing and mingling with several women and Gina found she was sexually attracted to a few of them. Gina noted, *"I was really excited. Some of the women were so sexy."*

A few of the women decided to go to the restroom and asked Gina to come along. Once inside, two of the women "attacked" her in the stall, kissing her and removing her panties to lick her pussy. *"I was fascinated with the whole thing. I really enjoyed it, but we were in there being bad girls and left the men in the club."* After she cleaned up and walked out of the bathroom, Martin was standing there with her coat. Remembering how that experience felt, he said, *"I was very upset with her. I felt like she hijacked our first experience."*

She had difficulty understanding why he would be so angry about women eating her pussy. But ultimately, she realized that he was upset because it was something they talked about experiencing together. Gina, embarrassed, said, *"He felt like I was being selfish and only cared about getting what I wanted. He wanted to share that moment with me but I took that away from him."*

Later that year, they went back to the club and met a redhead they both liked and took her back to their room to enjoy her. Gina found the shared experience with Martin immensely pleasurable. *"I loved being with a woman and my husband. I didn't know pussy could be so good."*

That experience left both of them longing for more.

They've secretly been in the Lifestyle for six years. Due to their careers, family, and children, they choose not to go public about how they conduct their relationship. The risk of losing their jobs and business connections is too high of a price to pay just so people would know they were non-monogamous. Predominantly, they go to LS events or parties and find women they are both interested in. They consider themselves swingers and only interested in having sex, with no emotional connections. Gina is very clear about her needs, *"I'm in it for the sex. I'm not interested in relationships with other people. I'm a 'hit and split' kind of girl. I already have his emotions to deal with, so I don't have time for some girl's emotions. Just come do what you came to do and hit the door."*

More recently they've explored adding men to the menu for Gina to enjoy. They could go full swap if the other couple or people in a group setting are fuckable enough. They haven't made clear agreements but have "settled into the flow," where they usually play together or are somewhere in the vicinity if the other is having sex. However, before anything occurs, they pull one another to the side to check in. *"We step out of the space to have a one-on-one conversation about what's going on. We don't speak for each other's bodies until we talk about it. Once we establish that we're both on board with a female or a couple, we act as a team to seal the deal."*

A short time ago, they came upon a touchy situation that forced them to establish some boundaries. They met a woman at an LS event that they fucked a few times. The woman lived in another state, so their interactions weren't frequent. Martin went on a trip with some friends and decided to go to the city where the woman resided. While at a nightclub, Martin ran into the other woman. Gina typically doesn't feel jealous or insecure when Martin is fucking other women, but this coincidental meeting left her feeling insecure because she felt like they decided to meet up without telling her. Although Martin didn't fuck the woman and maintains it was a coincidence, they've established an agreement that both of them must communicate any meetups with playmates beforehand. They love their restructured relationship. *"Our relationship doesn't stay the same. It's constantly evolving.*

As long as we're communicating, our relationship is pretty amazing."~ Gina & Martin est. 2002

Gina was intrigued about the endless sexual experiences she and Martin could have, so she made a choice to be honest with her husband and tell him about the scenarios she fantasized about. With the knowledge she obtained about the Lifestyle through her research, she felt they could be happier in a non-monogamous relationship. Both of them cheated at some point during the relationship, so it was clear to them that they needed fulfillment from others. Her husband agreed with her rationale and decided to give the Lifestyle a try. They more commonly seek sex from Unicorns and occasionally a Bull when the timing is right but will full swap if they meet a couple that they both agree are fuckable. After nineteen years, they are still going strong, happily married, and are enjoying every new adventure the Lifestyle has to offer.

Now I don't want to blow smoke up your ass and pretend like non-monogamy equates to happiness. Every Lifestyle relationship isn't peaches and cream. There are plenty of individuals in non-monogamous relationships who are just as miserable as those who are not. I eventually became unhappy in my open relationship as I realized that I wasn't getting what I really needed. I wanted to share my man in group sex situations, but all we really did was fuck other people separately. When you are in any relationship and doing things that don't make you feel complete, you will be extremely unhappy. Refusing to acknowledge that your relationship isn't ideal leads to sadness, depression, and misery.

Lyric and Jason met in 2005. They were both very Christian and very ready to find that special person to spend their lives with. By the time they met, Jason had already been knee-deep in the Lifestyle and knew that he wanted to be in a non-monogamous marriage if he was to ever get married. When he met Lyric, he felt like she could be the one to take his life to the next level, but he had deep desires that he didn't feel safe sharing with anyone besides his potential life partner. Like most men, Jason was infatuated with threesomes. The only difference was that he didn't care much for watching women with his woman; his dick got hard when he watched her get dominated by attractive men with big dicks. It wasn't something he was proud of, but it was who he was. He just needed to find the right time to tell Lyric before they got too serious.

A year and a half into their relationship, Jason decided to "come clean" and introduce Lyric to the Lifestyle. He had been conducting a secret life without her knowledge, but once marriage was possible, he knew it was time. He tricked lyric into attending her first Lifestyle party,

"One date night, I told her to dress sexy for a party I wanted to go to. I just didn't tell her the kind of party it was. But it was time for me to share that part of my life with her. Until then, I was doing it behind her back." Upon arrival, Lyric could tell that it was not an ordinary party. She recalled her reaction, *"I was shocked. People were mostly nude and having sex all around me. I had never been to a club like that before. I wondered why he brought me there."*

It was her first Lifestyle party, and although she was uncomfortable that night, she was able to have sex with Jason, but not with anyone else. An awkward few days passed before they discussed what happened that night. Lyric was curious to understand what that night was really about. Her initial question was an easy one, *"I asked him to help me understand what he was into because I didn't understand what was going on."*

Jason sat her down and explained to her what his deepest desires were. He recalled, *"I told her how much I loved threesomes, that I wanted to see her with women as well, but I preferred to have attractive men with big dicks fuck her. I let her know that if we were going to be together, this was going to be a part of our lives."* Lyric wasn't happy about knowing this part about the man she was planning to spend the rest of her life with. She struggled with her spirituality, *"I believed God sent me the man I was supposed to be with. So, I went along with it under the condition that I could control how often it happened. We made an agreement in advance that I could gradually minimize how often we did it until we were down to zero."* The plan was to decrease the frequency, hoping that one day he would have enough and be monogamous.

They got married five years later. They participated in LS activities twice per month until 2018. During that time, Lyric had developed a liking for women. She found that she enjoyed sex with women but not really with men. Lyric admitted, *"I prefer to have sex with women. I don't want to have sex with other men. Jason's dick is enough for me. He pleases me enough."* However, she continued to allow other men to fuck her because she knew doing so brought Jason an extreme amount of pleasure. Lyric continued with the behavior because it made Jason happy.

However, as time went on, she began to feel less and less good about herself and the things they were doing because they went against her Christian values. By 2020, she had minimized the frequency to four times per year. Yet, even with that, she was having a difficult time dealing with the guilt and shame she felt after their trysts were over. She looked as if she would cry and said, *"When our engagements end, I feel like trash, and I go into a depression. I don't feel like I'm doing the right thing. When bad things happen to me in my life, I think that God is punishing me for my behavior. I don't want to feel like that anymore. I want it to be just me and him, and that's it. I don't want to do this for the rest of our lives."*

Jason isn't happy with only having his needs fulfilled four times per year, but he also doesn't like that his wife is unhappy. Jason acknowledged the struggle, *"At first, she was cool with it, and we were having a good time.*

But I understand her need for me to pull away from it now. I'm not happy about that, but I love my wife more than I love the Lifestyle."

After eleven years of marriage, both of them have considered the consequences if he refuses to stop all Lifestyle activity. With Lyric almost at the end of her rope, she needs Jason to understand how serious she is about leaving the Lifestyle. She quietly stated, *"Divorce may be a consideration if it doesn't stop. We've discussed that. It's not what I want, but it is a possibility. I can't continue to live in sin."* ~ Lyric & Jason est. 2005

Both Jason and Lyric are unhappy in their current situation. When I spoke to her, she seemed very sad and withdrawn. As I watched her interact with others, she didn't talk to people, rarely smiled, and engaged with very few people besides Jason. As Lyric spoke about their relationship, Jason put his head down and sat quietly. As we discussed their issues, the tension between them was thick, and I could sense that it was a source of pain for both of them. On one hand, a wife loves her husband but is tired of being a part of his fantasies. She was not happy fucking other men and only did so to please him. She realizes that she may lose the love of her life if she refuses to allow him to live out his fantasies through her.

On the other hand, Jason has deep desires that have existed most of his life, but now his wife is asking him to stop being true to himself, ignore his innermost cravings, and be content with monogamous sex for the rest of their lives. I sympathize with both of them. Neither of them is right or wrong, they're just in a relationship that is no longer conducive for either of them, and unhappiness is the result.

Non-monogamous relationships are not immune to unhappiness; no relationship is. If you are unhappy, you either fix what's broken or cut your losses and move the fuck on. Being unhappy is never a good place to be, and that's why it's so important to understand that people and relationships evolve. Restructuring your relationship as you change becomes a necessary part of the growth of any relationship and is an integral step towards finding happiness. That happiness is attained when you are clear about your needs and specific with how you want to fulfill them. The way to accomplish that, specifically in non-monogamy, is by making agreements and setting reasonable and sustainable boundaries. Every non-monogamous relationship should go through this process. It is absolutely imperative if you want your new or restructured relationship to stand a chance.

AGREEMENTS
& BOUNDARIES

"You can't tell me how much time to take to fuck someone."

When my relationship began, my man and I decided that being open gave us the freedom we needed to feel sexually free and alive. Because of our desires to have sex with other people, we knew without that freedom, there was no relationship. I had been divorced for three years when we met. He had never been in love or had a serious relationship with anyone. I was the first woman he felt like he could be himself with, and he wanted to build a life with me. He was the first man I had shared my

true desires with and the first man I loved that I wanted to share with other
women.

As our open relationship was budding, it was important for us to create the boundaries that would guide how we interacted with other people. We made agreements that fulfilled our particular needs at that time, knowing we could change or tweak any of them when necessary. Both of us wanted to have a variety of sexual experiences with other people, and neither of us was interested in having any other emotional connections. At the core, our relationship would come before all others. We tailored our relationship specifically for us, as we wanted to experience it. Here are the agreements we made for our open relationship:

1. We only had sex with others. We didn't date them.

2. An initial date to establish fuckability was the only time dating occurred. Once fuckability was established, every subsequent meeting would be for sex.

3. If either of us felt like one of our playmates was catching feelings, it was up to us to discharge that playmate.

4. We did not attend Lifestyle events without the other present.

5. There were no sleepovers. We fucked and bounced.

We didn't have a limit on how many people either of us could fuck at any particular time. Unlike most Black couples, I was free to have sex with men and women of my choosing. We set aside specific days for playdates. We kept our weekends for us, but two other days during the week, we could arrange to have sex with someone else. We wanted to get to a point where we had more shared experiences than individual ones, but finding playmates that met our specific needs was very challenging.

Understand that this was the beginning of our relationship. Neither of us had experience in open relationships or non-monogamy, but we believed that what we agreed upon would be enough to keep our love and unity safe. However, I want you to look at our agreements and recognize what they are lacking. For one thing, these agreements were imposed on both of us equally, yet we were two different people who engaged in sex very differently. Secondly, there's no mention of how much time we could spend with playmates or whether or not we would introduce them to one another. There's also no mention of the level of intimacy that would be tolerable to witness between us and our playmates. Although my thoughts about time and intimacy have evolved, at that time, those things were important to me. Furthermore, our small list of agreements did not include boundaries at all. We just lumped everything into these five things, thinking we had it under control. By the time I had realized we had fallen short of controlling anything, it was too late.

We broke up about a year into our open relationship. I ended the relationship because he broke one of our agreements and refused to admit he had done anything wrong. One of our agreements was that we didn't date the people we were fucking. There was only one date to establish fuckabilty, and, after that, we only hooked up to fuck.

I had just moved to California temporarily for work, which he wasn't too happy about. Weeks before I left, we had an argument about both of us feeling unappreciated, which led to us feeling less connected. By the time I moved, we were somewhat disconnected emotionally and sexually.

I knew he was scheduled to fuck one of his lady friends the Friday after I left. That night, we talked on the phone until he pulled up to her home. After about three hours, I thought it was strange that I hadn't heard from him yet. Typically, he'd have his meet-up, fuck, and take off. Both of us would always call after we finished fucking, just to check in and chat about our sessions. It became our safety thing, the thing that reassured us that everything was going as agreed.

I called his phone, but he didn't answer. About an hour later, he called me, but he was still at the lady friend's place. That meant that for four hours, he was with this woman he was supposed to be just fucking. I was livid. For one, I fucked that man plenty, and I knew he didn't fuck for four hours. The dick was good, but he didn't fuck like that. Two, I wanted to know what the fuck they were doing when they weren't fucking. Our agreement stipulated that we weren't bonding or connecting with others. This was one of his main requests, that we don't bond or create opportunities where feelings could get in the way. We fucked, and that was that. So, what were he and this woman doing for four hours?

We began to discuss the matter while he was still with his lady friend. I asked him why he was still with her. He said that he needed a drink to relax so that he could fuck her. Apparently, she didn't have any alcohol at her place, so they decided to go to a bar nearby to have drinks. He said they stayed at the bar for two hours, went back to her place, fucked a couple of times, and then he called me. In my eyes, he admittedly broke our "no dating" agreement. Once they left her home to get drinks, they went out on a date: agreement broken. From his perspective, he did what he had to do to relax to fuck the woman. He felt like his actions were justified because it was what he needed at the time. No, "You're right, babe. I should've grabbed a drink before I got there." No, "I'm sorry, babe. I'll be more prepared next time so that it doesn't happen again." Nothing that was remotely remorseful about his actions. He couldn't acknowledge he had done anything wrong. He couldn't accept that I felt like he betrayed my trust, and he refused to apologize. So, I broke it off. Not because of what he did; going to the bar with the woman was not only an excusable offense, it was also the first time we had an issue like that. I ended it because he couldn't acknowledge that he was wrong, and for me, that was *intolerable. In any relationship, you have to be willing to say, "I'm sorry. I fucked up." Because you will fuck up.*

We never stood a chance. Not without first establishing certain boundaries around how long a playdate should be or whether or not it was okay to step out if the situation in the home was not ideal. That was something we never discussed because it never was an issue. In that moment, I felt like four hours was too long to spend with a person if you're just having sex. When I said as much, he responded, *"You can't tell me how much time to take to fuck someone."* The argument continued to roll downhill when the reality is that it didn't have to. I was emotional and feeling betrayed and he was too stubborn to apologize to ease the burning feelings raging inside me. We had never gone through any issues that involved other people so we were ill-equipped to handle unforeseen issues, and we were incapable of communicating with one another effectively once we felt injured. We also never made an agreement about when to discuss issues that may arise or how to handle them. We should have created an agreement that when we felt injured, we would first clear our heads, then revisit the situation with less hurt and anger involved. Instead, we powered through the argument, pointing fingers and making accusations until I gave up and said "I'm done".

After the relationship ended, I realized most of our agreements had more to do with our insecurities, rather than actualizing our happiness. Neither one of us wanted to create opportunities for playmates to catch feelings so we thought operating like robots, with no emotions, was the right decision. But I was unhappy moving that way, and the men I fucked or attempted to fuck said that I was cold and distant which turned them off. I realized that I missed creating connections with lovers because it enhanced my sexual experiences with them. It can't be all dick and pussy but no smiles or hugs. We were immature from a non-monogamous perspective and allowed our insecurities about losing one another dictate how we should behave when interacting with other people.

I want you to do better than me. Once you decide to start your Lifestyle journey, I want you to create an Affirmation List that clearly outlines your specific needs, things that would make you uncomfortable, and things that would be absolutely intolerable. Be as honest and introspective as you can be. Don't worry about how you may appear or whether or not your partner will agree. Have your partner do the same. From there, you can establish boundaries and make agreements that will help you feel safe and secure in unfamiliar territory.

Your Affirmation list could look something like this:

* I need:

To feel safe and secure in this relationship.

You to listen to me when I feel insecure or hurt.

You to try to see things from my perspective even when you disagree.

To have a variety of sex partners.

To have sex with men and women.

To be present when you're having sex with others.

For us to have shared sexual experiences.

To feel loved by you and my other partners.

To feel safe enough to talk to you about anything that bothers me.

To be heard and not minimized when I talk to you about my feelings.

You to respect the agreements we've made.

You to talk to me if you want to change anything that we've agreed upon.

*   I would be uncomfortable:

If you stayed out all night with a playmate and didn't call.

If you only wanted to have sex with others when I wasn't present.

If you only wanted to go to LS events with other women.

If you didn't want to share me with the women you regularly fuck.

If you kissed your playmates passionately.

If you shared our secrets with your playmates.

If you told me you loved someone else and wanted to spend more time with that person.

If you don't share your experiences with me.

If you tell me too much about your experiences.

If your playmates didn't want to meet me.

*   It would be intolerable:

If you lie to me.

If you break our agreements and didn't acknowledge that you made a mistake.

If you can't apologize when you do wrong.

If you don't listen to me when I'm talking to you about my feelings.

If you laugh at my concerns or insecurities and minimize me or call me names.

If you pick a fight every time I'm scheduled to meet up with a playmate.

If you have unprotected sex with anyone besides me.

If you made plans with me but then canceled to meet up with someone else.

I'm sure you can feel how uncomfortable discussing these issues could be. These are some of the things you can include in your Affirmation List if they apply to you. From here, you can begin to create boundaries and make agreements that would be achievable for both of you. Keep in mind that these agreements do not have to be equal. For instance, your partner may be okay with you regularly fucking a playmate, as long as they are introduced, whereas you may not want to be involved with your partner's playmates at all.

The agreements shouldn't be "one for you, and one for me." They should be tailored specifically for what each of you wants and needs. Don't be afraid to keep it a hundred. A closed mouth don't get fed. If you fail to convey your deepest desires or your most terrifying concerns, you will lose in the end, and it'll be your fault. You can't expect your partner to read your mind. Now, you won't be able to think of every situation that may become problematic. Sometimes it takes for a thing to happen for you to realize just how bothered you are. The important thing is that you agree to time and space where either of you has the opportunity to discuss your feelings or concerns and amend agreements and boundaries when necessary. You probably won't get it right at the very beginning. Very few people do. Non-monogamous relationships are like ordinary ones. They take time, understanding, and your ability to communicate your needs effectively. Understanding this will help you create agreements that will make both of you very happy and, hopefully, keep you well fucked.

How to Share Your Man

"You do not own his heart, his mind, or his dick."

O n New Year's Day, I shared my man with a gorgeous woman, she, in turn, shared her husband with me. It was our first successful full swap with a highly fuckable couple. Most times, when my man and I had sex with others, we did it separately. But my true desire was to share him with other women and be shared by him with other men. I love group sex and wanted to fuck people who wanted to fuck both of us together. It was challenging to find attractive and physically compatible Black people to fuck. Still, it was even harder finding Black couples that allowed penetration of the wife by another man. So, when we came across a full swap, sexy, Black couple, we were super geeked. We preferred to fuck full swap couples. There's nothing worse than a husband who won't allow another dick in his wife but is ready to dick down another man's woman. I would never fuck someone's man if the man I'm with can't also fuck. So, when we dealt with couples, it was an even swap or nothing at all.

They both rated high on our fuckability scale. The wife was thick, with a fat ass and a cute face. Her husband was tall and attractive. She was very flirty with my man but made it known that she was interested in both men and women. This was a win because it meant that both of us would be getting the pussy. It also meant new dick for me, and I love new dick. Both of us really wanted the wife. The optics had us very excited. She and I have elaborate back tattoos, so my dude was excited for the moment when he looked down as we sucked his dick at the same time. I wanted to taste her pussy, then watch her squirm as he dicked her down real good. The idea of fucking both of us made his dick hard, and I was definitely going to get him what he wanted. The husband was an added bonus I was grateful to receive, but he just went along with whatever she wanted to do. His sex energy was low, and his passive disposition made his presence futile.

After drinks at a bar, we met up at my place. As the men made drinks, I stripped naked and encouraged her to do the same. She was embarrassed because she wasn't properly groomed. So, I took her to the bathroom, ran a hot bath, and shaved her in the tub while the men watched. I love a bald pussy, and once she was hairless, I started licking her tender lips. The men were getting restless watching us play alone together so I tasted her a bit more then grabbed towels to dry us off. Once we dried off and entered my room, I pushed her down on the bed, spread her legs, and continued to suck her sweet flesh. I love the taste of clean pussy. I find it highly erogenous and as I licked her, her own juices started to flow. The fragrant scent of her excited me and I started getting wet. As we played, the men tired of watching and joined us. Mine was eager and slid inside me from behind while she sucked her husband's dick. Soon after, I slid over so my man could have his turn with her.

While he continued what I started, I eagerly grabbed her husband's dick and wrapped my lips around it. I squatted over her face and dropped my pussy on her mouth. While she licked me, my dude slid on a condom and entered her. I could hear the surprise in her voice as she gasped for breath. I turned around and kissed her, dampening her moans as he fucked her. The husband followed suit. He slid on a condom and started to fuck me while I watched my man enjoy fucking his wife. Mine leaned in and kissed me passionately as he slid in and out of her. Eventually, I needed to feel him inside me, so we switched partners. I lay on my back. He then frogged my legs and fucked me deep and hard. I knew I was close to cumming, but I wanted to do so with my tongue in her pussy. So I flipped over, pulled her to me, spread her legs, and tasted more of her. Her husband slid his dick into her mouth, while mine banged me out until I came. After I climaxed, I moved out of the way so he could gift her with the same. He was very well endowed; long and girthy. Women tended to struggle beneath his thrusts and I loved to watch him find pleasure in making them take all he had to offer. He watched me as he fucked her deep and hard. "Take all of that dick", I whispered repeatedly into her ear and kissed her neck. She moaned and squirmed beneath his firm thrusts until she came. Meanwhile, I let the husband fuck me more, but I knew my man wanted to cum inside me. So she and I squirmed over to our partners and let them finish the way they loved to – in hot, wet, juicy pussy.

The belief that no woman is truly comfortable or happy sharing her man with other women is simply not true. Obviously, some women would never consider it, but there are others who absolutely love it! Sharing your man is an art form that requires making the conscious decision to be selfless and place his happiness above your insecurities. This is not an easy thing to do, especially when most of us feel insecure when we are in a vulnerable state. However, you must understand that your insecurities are derived from negative beliefs you have about yourself that are most likely untrue. If you focus on whether or not another woman looks better than, smells better than, or feels better than you, you will never be sexually freed, and you'll be stuck in the same type of relationships wondering why your man can't keep his dick in his pants.

Sharing your man and other Lifestyle pursuits is not for everyone. I will tell you that you need to have a good relationship that is built on loyalty, trust, and respect in order for non-monogamy to be successful. If you don't have a healthy relationship, attempting to share your man would be a disaster. People say if your relationship is good, then why do it? Well, if your relationship is so good, why not? Believe it or not, most people feel trapped in monogamous relationships, men more so than women. When you deny the right to choose to do what one pleases with one's own body, a sense of confinement emerges. Those feelings of confinement are related to repressed thoughts and behaviors that would normally make us happy when we're not in restricted relationships.

Imagine now that you put non-monogamy on the table as an option for your relationship. A man who is true to the idea of releasing himself from monogamous norms would feel as if you freed him. Do you realize the sizeable burden that would be released from him if you allowed him to be free? Think about it! You would be saying yes to the one thing he was told he could never have when in a relationship: extra pussy. You would not only allow him to actualize his sexual fantasies, but you would also bear witness to the part of him he always kept hidden in his other relationships. Until you, he lied to practically every woman he met about his true desires and cheated on most of them. The lying and the cheating are definitely shortcomings of his, but if you opened the door for him to walk through as his true self, it would change how he related to you, physically and emotionally.

I thoroughly enjoyed sharing my man. In fact, I can't determine which part I liked better. Was it that I enjoyed watching him please another woman while I also gave and received pleasure from her? Was it that he was happy, and he knew his happiness was important to me? Or was it because sharing him brought us closer together, and he felt comfortable to be himself in our relationship? I can't truly say, but there is something highly erotic about sharing my lovers. When I understand what my man finds pleasurable and help bring his fantasies to fruition, it creates an erogenous feeling inside me that is unmatched.

I believe that each of us deserves to have *exactly* what we desire in life. Who and how we fuck should not be exempt from that. Sex is supposed to be fun and immensely pleasurable. Why would you stop someone you love from having that? It's hypocrisy to say you would do anything to make your man happy, then in the same breath say, your pussy is the last he'll ever touch. That is definitely not going to make him happy. The saying, *"If he loved you the way you loved him, he would want you and only you"*, is not only based on a narrative that is untrue and damaging to your relationships, it is also built on the false premise that somehow people become your property once feelings are involved. It's this sense of possession over others that has most people unable to accept that we can share ourselves and still be loyal to the relationship, however it's fashioned. Before you choose to share your man's body, affection, and love with other women, you must understand that you do not possess him. He does not belong to you, nor you to him. You do not own his heart, his mind, or his dick. He makes a conscious decision to share himself with you, but how much he shares depends on your level of acceptance of who he really is.

We decide to share ourselves with whomever we choose. How or why you choose to move into a "sharing is caring" space is up to you. The practice of non-monogamy may not have been a viable option for you until now. When you don't understand how or why people end up in relationships that look very different from yours, it's easy to turn your nose up and pass judgment. When August Alsina came out publicly about his relationship with Jada Pinkett Smith, people had both positive and negative things to say about the nature of their relationship. We'll never know the truth of the situation, but it doesn't matter at the end of the day. People have the right to do as they please in their relationship without the judgments of our do-gooder society. When you decide to invite other women into your bed, you have to determine whether it's right for you.

Women who are sexually attracted to other women have an easier time transitioning into non-monogamy. Oftentimes women who like women can accept their man having additional lovers because they may also benefit sexually or emotionally from those interactions. Yet, sex is not the only reason a woman agrees to share her man with other women. Sometimes it's just pure selflessness and an understanding that her man has needs she can't meet, or perhaps she's just tired of fucking him and wouldn't mind someone else taking on the burden. It may sound strange but sharing your man may be an option if you find yourself in any one of the following positions.

* **You are Bi**. You are interested in having sex with women, so the idea of him fucking another woman and both of them receiving pleasure from you turns you on. You can be either Bi-curious, Bi-friendly, or Bi-sexual, and you simply have the desire to share him physically and/or emotionally with other women because it's a source of gratification for you. These interactions can be strictly for sex, or you can agree to have short or long-term relationships. Either way, both of you fulfill your need to have sexual experiences with other women.

Tasha, DC ~ *"I knew I was attracted to women but never had a sexual experience with one. I told my husband I would like to try a threesome someday. He was definitely into the idea. We just needed to figure out with whom and how it would happen. One date night,* *we decided to try to find someone who would be interested in having sex with both of us. We heard about a sex club nearby and decided to go. We met a really attractive woman that was interested in having sex with us. So we took her to one of the private playrooms because I wasn't yet comfortable being watched. Once we locked the door, she kissed me on my mouth and immediately went down on me. It was the best thing I'd felt in a long time. Within a few minutes, I came. My husband was very excited. His dick was rock hard, and he jerked it as he watched us. I wanted to go down on her to see what it was like, so I licked her a little, but I don't think I was very good at it. I could see her watching my husband in the corner, so I waved him over to us. I spread her legs open as my husband tasted her just before he dove right in. As he fucked her, I tried to lick her clit to help her cum. The more she moaned, the harder he fucked her until he was ready to explode. When he was about to climax, he pulled out of her, took the condom off, and jammed his dick into my mouth. As he let loose, I rubbed on her clit until she came too. I don't know who had more fun that night. But my cherry was popped, and that club became one of our favorite date night spots."*

* **You know your man wants other pussy, and you want to gift it to him.** You enjoy how happy he is when he can have more than just you. In turn, he appreciates that you understand his need for variety. This gift doesn't have to be an everyday thing. But you offer him opportunities to get what he needs from other women. You agree to these interactions and you can choose whether or not to be a part of them.

Kim, Atlanta ~ *"My boyfriend mentioned having a threesome with me and another woman a few times. I wasn't interested in touching a woman, so I wasn't sure how we could have one. I didn't believe that* *we were meant to be with only one person forever, but I hadn't met a guy interested in some of the things I heard about people doing. I thought that having sex with two men would be cool, but he didn't like that idea. I also liked to watch live sex rather than recorded porn, so I told him I would be okay with him having sex with another woman as long as I could watch. The first time it happened, I really just observed. The woman was okay with me watching because she was an exhibitionist and liked people watching her fuck. While he fucked her, I was so turned on I started to masturbate. After they finished and she left, I and my boyfriend had the most amazing sex. Now we go places where finding women for him to have sex with while I watch, is normal behavior.»*

* **You have a low sex drive and can't match his libido.** Sharing him with another woman can be helpful by easing your burden to fulfill his sexual needs all of the time. Imagine having a man that wants sex daily, but you no longer desire sex as frequently. He is not going to be fulfilled or happy in that relationship. Granting him a pass to have sex with other women could help keep him sexually satisfied and ultimately save your relationship.

Dee, Philly ~ *"My partner and I have been together for fifteen years. For the first 5-7 years, we had sex all of the time. It was great. But after we started having kids, I was less and less interested in it. He wanted to have sex often, but if it wasn't on a scheduled day I planned and prepared for, I didn't want to do it. I knew he was getting antsy and maybe even cheated on me. It hurt me to think about it, but if I was being honest with myself, I knew I couldn't please him. It was a hard pill to swallow. I did some research on this kind of thing and decided if I loved him, it wasn't fair to expect him to ignore his hunger for sex when I knew I couldn't keep him satisfied. I was willing* *to allow him to have other women, but I didn't know how to handle my jealous and insecure thoughts. I also didn't want to lose him to another woman. After many heartfelt discussions, we agreed that he could find partners to satisfy his sexual needs, but they couldn't be women he had serious relationships with in the past. I couldn't manage knowing he was having sex with a woman he once loved."*

✳ **You don't want to have children, but he wants to start a family or have a bigger one.** Sharing your man with a woman who is willing to love him and bear him children would provide him with the family he wants while maintaining his relationship with you. If you already have children, both of you could be bonus moms for all of the children. The relationship between the three of you could become one that is nurturing and fulfilling for all involved.

Shannon, Brooklyn ~ *"I've been married to my husband more than twenty years now. Our relationship started with just the two of us and our children, but after ten years, my husband talked about having more children. I knew I no longer wanted to give birth to any more little humans, so I suggested finding someone who would. Our relationship was great, but he's full of energy and has a big heart, so I was happy to share him with someone else. We searched for a while and eventually found a beautiful young woman willing to be in a relationship with us and give him the children he desired. She and I became very close and eventually became lovers as well. We refer to one another as sister wives. However, we're less like sisters than we are wives. She's very special to me and blessed us with two beautiful children, whom I love like my own. After several years, we brought in a third sister wife and formed a quad, which was fun for a while, but eventually became too much to deal with. We found our happy* *place with the three of us and our children, and now grandchildren. My husband is still full of energy and gets together with his other playmates from time to time. Now and then, we join him for some of his little trysts, but we're comfortable in our space as wives, mamas, and grands."*

These are just a few testimonials from Black women that decided to be in non-monogamous relationships. Each of them willingly chose to participate in relationships that were more beneficial to both partners. It's common for people to believe that there's something wrong with women in non-monogamous relationships or that they were coerced or forced into sharing their partners. But what it really comes down to is personal choice and individual happiness. If you know that you could never be happy with sharing any part of your man with another woman, it is best to stay away from the Lifestyle in general. If you're still struggling with the idea, but can see the potential of having a non-monogamous relationship, begin having the conversations with your partner to get a better idea of what you and he are comfortable doing. In the beginning, it won't be perfect. Both you and your man will make mistakes. But if you have a solid foundation and open communication you can get through the most difficult parts.

Some of the most challenging things to do are to acknowledge your weaknesses and control your emotions. You may not know you're a jealous woman until you watch your man dick down another woman and make her cum. Understanding your triggers and how to handle your thoughts and behaviors when you're feeling insecure or jealous will be vital to the success of your relationship.

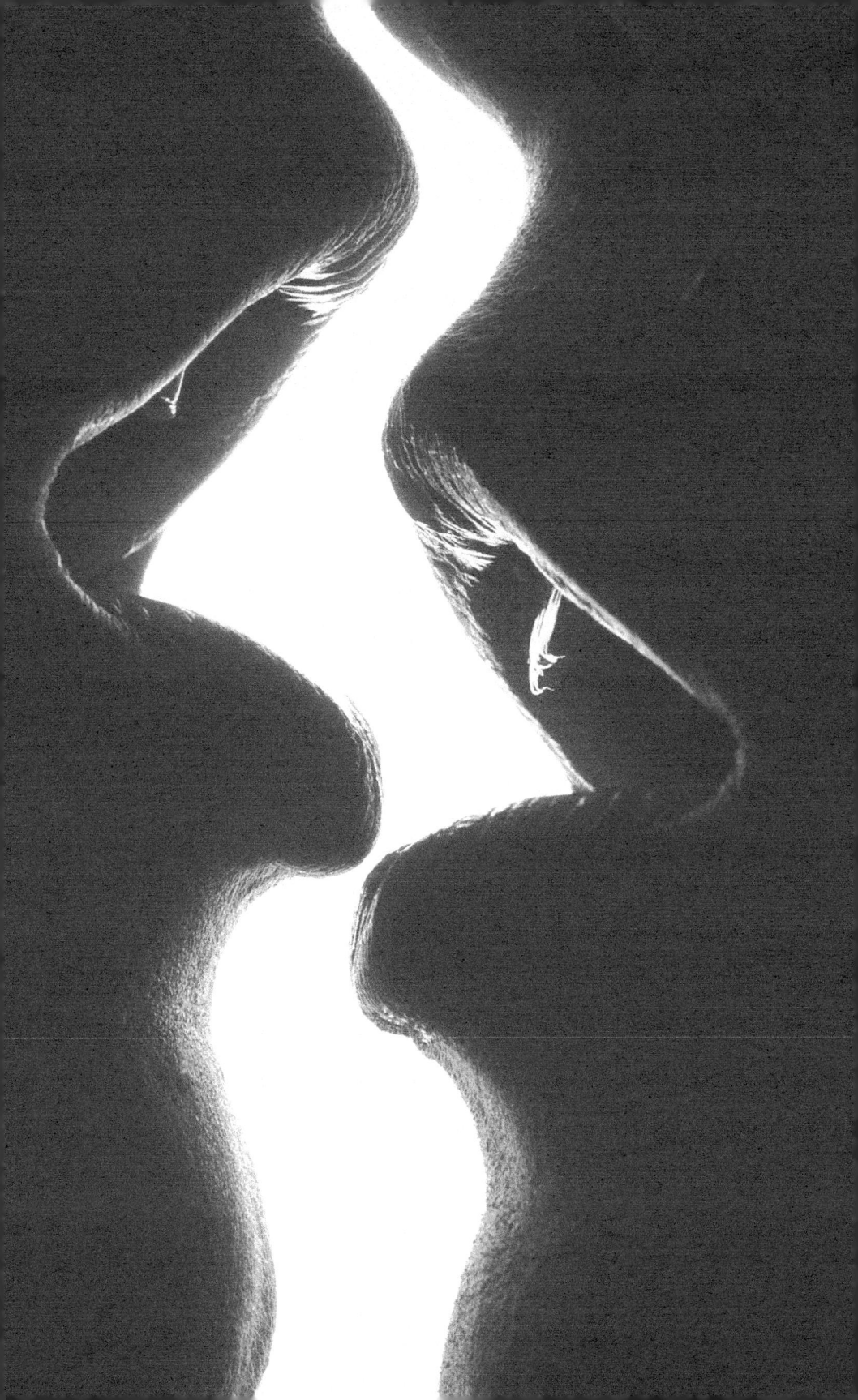

INSECURITY & JEALOUSY: YOUR WORST ENEMIES

"I had no idea how to share my man with others and allow connections to happen, without the fear of losing him."

I didn't like that other women required so much attention from my man in order to fuck him. I didn't care about what he did with his dick, but I didn't like when he shared parts of him I believed were for me. I watched him hold hands and lock fingers with a woman after we fucked, and I didn't like that at all. I immediately stopped them and killed the whole vibe. I didn't like that some of his playmates wanted a set day each week for them to fuck him. I felt like that was too permanent of an arrangement, so I shot that *down. Another one wanted him to be her partner at a sex club, but I didn't want him to go to those environments without me, especially not with some other woman. When he had sex with playmates without me, I would sometimes wonder how intimate he was with the other women. Was he holding them and loving on them after they fuck? Does he spend hours talking on the phone, getting to know them when I'm not around? Was he really telling them about me and the agreements of our relationship? Thoughts like these would give me anxiety and cause me to question my relationship with him.*

At that time, the whole open relationship thing was new to me. The sex didn't bother me, but I believed that any emotional connection he had should be with me and me alone. I had no idea how to share my man with others and allow connections to happen without the fear of losing him. Both of us shared the same fear, which led to our agreement that we "just fucked" and didn't date. When I had sex with my playmates, I didn't leave room for any type of connection, fearing that doing so would be a betrayal of trust. Thinking back on it now, it was kind of silly, expecting people to be satisfied with just fucking and no chance at all to connect with us. I didn't realize how silly our agreement was until after the relationship ended. Later, I understood that most people needed to feel some type of connection in order to have sex, some more than others. However, I couldn't come to terms with that at that time. I was so focused on protecting my insecure heart that I never stopped to ask what I was afraid of losing if he happened to connect with someone else. That fear ultimately led to feelings of jealousy and negative thoughts which were damaging to our relationship.

Insecure and jealous individuals do not make good Lifestyle partners or playmates. If you are generally an insecure person, the Lifestyle isn't the place for you. If you are not in control of your emotions, you will not be able to control the behavior that results from those feelings, and your relationship will not survive. Both partners must be whole, and the relationship must be strong if you plan to practice non-monogamy. If you think you will always be the hottest, have the best body, or fuck your partner better than anyone, you're setting yourself up for failure. There is no way to control what someone else looks like or may feel like. Those things are out of your control. Rest assured, there will be times when you will feel insecure, but the idea is not to let those insecurities lead you to behave in a way that is detrimental to your relationship.

I struggled a bit with feeling secure in my open relationship. I am not typically an insecure or jealous person, and I rarely feel anxious about anything. However, due to my lack of experience in non-monogamous relationships, I tapped into those emotions. Shortly before we broke up, we weren't communicating effectively. Not just about the sexual things, but about the relationship in general. I felt disconnected and unsure about the validity of our love and ultimately felt less secure about our relationship. He wasn't in a space to provide me with reassurances, so I didn't feel safe enough to voice my concerns. Instead, I kept quiet, and the negative feelings festered. As more and more things transpired, my feelings were becoming harder to control. I started having insecure thoughts about being replaced by another woman. This led me to question his integrity, and, eventually, I felt I could no longer trust him. By the time the incident happened with the other woman (when he went out for drinks and spent over four hours with her), I wasn't willing to accept anything except an acknowledgment of wrongdoing and an apology. When I didn't get one, I blew up and ended it all.

In reality, I didn't end it because of what he did. I ended it because I felt exposed and grossly vulnerable, and I didn't like who I was becoming. I wasn't comfortable in the space of the unknown, a position I put myself in because I was too afraid to speak up when something troubled me. This is why open and effective communication is a must. You must address things that make you uncomfortable to prevent your insecure and jealous feelings from becoming problematic. Ask for reassurances from your partner if and when you need them. Don't end up bitter, unapproachable, or fake like some of the people I've encountered in Lifestyle environments.

It's easy to spot the insecure and jealous people in the Lifestyle, especially the women. Although men are insecure and get jealous, they rarely show their emotions in that environment. Typically, a couple knows what they're looking for and the man either catches what they want himself or sits back and lets his woman do the fishing. The women, on the other hand, are transparent as fuck. They're usually the ones with the nasty attitude that barely speak even when you say hello. When you catch her watching you from a distance, she gives you the fake half-smile and raised eyebrows. She's the one with hella rules and restrictions placed on her man. He can't do shit without her feeling some type of way. If you approach them, she takes his hand or locks their arms to let you know that he's her man. If her man likes you, no matter how often she says, *"It's okay for you to fuck my man,"* she will never let you give him the pussy. If she's single, she's the one that gets mad when the dude or chick she has her eye on is entertaining other attractive women. If she isn't the center of attention, she takes it personally and will most likely let you know it once you circle back around to her. She'll say things like, *"I saw you talking to your little friend."* Girl bye! Nobody has time for that energy when they're trying to fuck. Watch out for these annoying ass women; they're usually fronting and not with the fuckery anyway. They pretend like the LS environment is for them, but inside they're secretly hating while wishing they could be someone else. If you see your likeness in any of these women, please work on yourself first before attempting non-monogamy or entering the LS scene.

*   **Jealous Jada:** This woman really wants to be in a monogamous relationship, but the man she loves wants them to be with other women. She obliges to keep him but has very little interest in licking pussy and does not find pleasure in watching her man dick down other women. She doesn't like the attention he shows

other women, so she gets an attitude and becomes unapproach-able. She only notices when attractive women are around because she knows he also sees those women. She always has an attitude or "stank" face and has a hard time having a good time if she can't keep both eyes on him. She thinks that women have an agenda to steal her man, so she's always playing defense. She will stir up negative energy to pick a fight with him in order to tame his behavior hoping he won't be in the mood to deal with other women. If her man gets too excited about fucking a woman she believes is "above" her, she will do anything to ensure that they never connect. It's difficult for her to accept that a woman is genuinely attracted to them strictly for the purpose of sex and nothing more.

* **Insecure Imani:** This woman has a hard time accepting that his love for her is not diminished by sex with others. She is usually harsh when judging herself and secretly wants to look and be dif-ferent. She can't really understand why he desires other women, so she internalizes it to mean something is wrong with her. She gets irritable when attractive women are around because she consistently compares herself to them. She only befriends women who she thinks are on her level or beneath her because they make her feel better about herself. She tries to act like she's a bad bitch, but inside she wishes she was someone else. She permits her man to fuck others but creates rules for him that are hella restricting and controlling. For instance, he can't cum while fucking anyone besides her, or he can only fuck women that she chooses. She may or may not desire women but if she does, she only wants women who are more into her than her man and actually prefers women whose preference is also women.

Now, I'm not here to tell you how to conduct your relationship, but I would caution you against being or bringing a Jada or Imani into your bed. They are no fun at all and impossible to deal with. They are as dull as the day is long and a buzz kill at any LS event. Instead of having a great time, Jada and Imani will sit around with their bad attitudes, throwing shade on women that intimidate them, complaining about any and everything.

Men are not exempt, they also struggle with jealousy and insecurity, even if they don't publicly display these emotions. They tend to be insecure when their woman wants to fuck a man who is better looking, taller, or has a bigger dick than him. The "big dick" part is the hardest to deal with because if he isn't as well-endowed as the other man, the belief is that his woman will always desire the other man's dick. Men also get jealous of other women when they don't feel tended to by their women. Some men want to be the focus of attention in a group sex situation and will feel slighted if it doesn't turn out the way they expected.

* **Joe, Bronx** ~ *"My wife and I have been together for eighteen years. Married for almost six of them. We started having threesomes two years before we got married. The threesomes started kind of soft play because she wasn't comfortable with me penetrating another woman. Our first threesome was cool but we fell out and had a huge argument. During the threesome, the other woman gave me head, and I returned the favor. When my wife got more comfortable she let the woman give her head then she went down on the woman. Once they got started, they were really into it with each other. After it was over, my wife was upset with me because I touched the women, in a threesome no less. I didn't know that giving the woman head would be off-limits for me. My wife didn't know either until she witnessed it. She also didn't know how much she would enjoy being with a woman. It was something we dis-cussed over the years, but never something she experienced until the*

threesome. However, once she was into it, she was really into it, and she had no idea how bad she had it for women until she got a taste. She was into it so much that she forgot I was even there. It was almost as if she wanted the girl to herself, which made me feel some type of way. To be honest, I felt vulnerable and insecure because I didn't feel included at all. So both of us had our own issues after the first time. The second time we tried a threesome it went more smoothly. The only difference was that I fucked the other woman and I fucked her good. It was the first time my wife witnessed me fucking another woman, and she didn't like the way she felt watching it. She got mad again and we had another huge argument. This one was harder to move on from, but we got through it.

Eventually, we were able to have threesomes without a whole lot of drama, although the issues that came up later weren't about the sex. She had a problem with trying to control me and everything else. She questioned me about everything. She had a problem with the level of intimacy between me and the others and she didn't want me communicating with the women we were engaging in sex with. Somehow, she thought we would just have sex with these women, but wouldn't talk to them about anything else. I tried to get her to understand that it didn't work that way. She just wanted to fuck them and be done, but I wanted it to be a regular thing. She then began to express her desire to have sex with other men. I didn't like it, but I understood. Some part of me sees her as property, so watching another man get my pussy would be really hard. But I know it would be selfish of me not to let her get what she needs. I just know I wouldn't be turned on by it, and it would be really difficult to watch."

Insecurity and jealousy are your worst enemies and will destroy your relationship if you don't learn how to control them. Both men and women grapple with these emotions so it's important to understand what your triggers are and how to deal with the emotions that follow once they're sparked. It's also crucial to the relationship to understand your partner's triggers, how your partner feels and what your partner needs to ensure that things go as smoothly as possible. Once you have a better understanding of how to manage your jealousy, you can tailor your relationship according to the unique issues that trigger them. This way both of you will be on the same page and can discuss the jealous feelings without judgment. Being on the same page includes having clear agreements and setting boundaries that keep you both feeling safe and validated. When the two of you aren't on the same page, problems will arise that could potentially lead to disaster if you aren't openly communicating your feelings.

If you battle with insecurities and jealousy, yet non-monogamy and the Lifestyle culture resonates with you, then you have some self-actualization work to do before opening your relationship to other people. Working to self-actualize requires you to:

* **Love and understand yourself**
* **Practice acceptance of life's many wonders**
* **Live life authentically in your truth**
* **Understand what you need to gain fulfillment**
* **Feel secure and unashamed of who you truly are**

This work must be done by you and you alone. Self-help books, videos, and therapy are all useful devices to help you achieve self-actualization. However, it is you who has to be willing to accept that it is time for a change. If you are on the fence about entering the Lifestyle, but you know it's something you and your partner are willing to try, getting to a point where you are relaxed and secure in that space will help you find pleasure in those experiences.

How do you get comfortable with the idea of your partner fucking someone else? The honest truth is, your comfort level increases when you feel safe and supported during the process. The jealous feelings will lessen over time, but this can only happen when you engage in honest communication. If you can't communicate effectively, it will be impossible to fully explore your sexuality and enjoy the Lifestyle. Great communication begins by conveying your need for safety as well as your need to feel heard in your relationship. Considering you've agreed to open your bedroom door to let other people in, it's important that you are given the space to feel jealous, hurt, or insecure, but it's equally as important to know how to dampen those feelings. Both of you must be willing to listen to any concerns and offer comfort when needed. But at some point, you have to figure out a way to deal with these emotions without your partner's help. It wouldn't be fair to either of you if you agreed to fucking other people, but then had a problem every time there's a scheduled meet-up with a playmate.

One of the best tools to use when struggling with insecurity and jealousy in the moment is an Emotions Check. An Emotions Check is a moment you take to sit still, be silent, and try to understand why you're feeling the way you do. When you do this, you slow down the barrage of chaotic thoughts and feelings, and you run through a simple checklist before reacting.

- ✓ **How do I feel?** Are you hurt, angry, jealous? Do you feel like you're losing?

- ✓ **Why do I feel this way?** Are your feelings fueled by your insecurities or do you have a legitimate reason to be upset?

- ✓ **Do I believe it was my partner's intention to hurt me?** Was the thing that occurred something that could have been avoided or done differently? Is this the first time it happened?

✓ **How do I communicate my feelings?** Remain calm. Don't do or say anything irrational. Ask for a moment to sit down and have a conversation with your partner. Use "I" statements rather than "you" accusations. Cry if you need to. Ask for reassurances. Trust the process.

An Emotions Check can be used in any situation but will be a very useful tool as you navigate within the Lifestyle. You should not judge yourself too harshly about feeling insecure or jealous. It happens to the best of us. Just do whatever it takes to let go of the ideas and beliefs that nurture your emotions, and you'll have the tools you need to conquer any situation. Remember, it only takes one negative experience for your partner to mistrust you or to associate negative feelings about your choice to be non-monogamous. Regaining that trust can be a long battle, so make every effort to ensure you abide by the agreements and respect the boundaries that you and your partner create.

THE DOUBLE STANDARD

**"A woman's sexual desires are no less
important than a man's."**

We aren't meant to be with one person for the rest of our lives," says practically every man. The problem with that opinion is that usually when men say "we," what they really mean is men, not women. In other words, men aren't meant to be monogamous, but women are. A woman is expected to accept that her man needs other pussy, help him obtain other pussy, and even stand by while he conducts a full-blown relationship with another woman. Meanwhile, he refuses to allow her to have other dick. A woman is expected not to feel insecure, to be open and support-ive, and give him the space to feel happy, while he exercises his freedom to fulfill his needs. Yet, that same man will deny his woman the same freedoms.

This double standard exists in the minds of many men, but it really permeates throughout Black culture. This is where non-monogamy gets lost with Black people and why so many Black women are afraid to speak their truth.

Plenty of Black women accept and agree that non-monogamy can lead to more fulfilling relationships. The idea of having the kind of love they seek while also having pleasurable experiences with other people turns them on. Yet it is uncommon for them to openly verbalize this to their partners. Why? Because many of them aren't bi and don't want to have sex with other women. What they really want is to fuck other men, but they are too afraid to admit it. They are afraid to be honest about their desires for other dick out of fear of being rejected and alone. When a woman is interested in having sex with multiple partners, and she vocalizes that, most men no longer see her as "wifey" material and they scurry away. Thus, if marriage is the goal, the average woman will not risk the opportunity for lifelong partnership by being honest about her true sexual nature. A lot of men are delusional and really believe that one dick is enough for any woman. It's a lie they tell themselves to avoid dealing with the truth. Men say they want the truth, but they can't handle the fucking truth! Instead, they have created false narratives to rationalize why women should be monogamous and content with one dick.

"God created women to be helpmates for men, not the other way around."

"Women are emotional beings."

"Women have sex with their hearts."

"Women can't separate emotion from sex."

"Women are internal beings. They receive sex. They don't give it."

Blah. Blah. Blah. It's all a bunch of bullshit if you ask me. Men love to use a woman's "emotional state" to deem her unfit for extra-partner fucking with other men. They put on airs as if a woman can't handle other dick, as if somehow a woman is hard-wired to be monogamous. But the truth is that men can't handle the idea of another man fucking a woman they have emotional attachments to. They would share a friend with benefits (FWB) at the drop of a dime. But a woman they feel connected to? Forget about it! I find this ideology interesting and disturbing at the same time. So, I questioned several men who practice non-monogamy about why they don't share their women with other men. This is what they had to say:

> **Jay, Bmore** ~ *"I can't be in a relationship with a woman if she's having sex with other men. Once another man enters her, she carries his masculine energy with her, and there can't be any other masculine energy but mine."*
>
> **Marc, Htown** ~ *"I can't get hard if she's having sex with another man. If his dick is bigger than mine, and he fucks her good, she might keep thinking about that dude when I'm fucking her."*
>
> **Ant, Queens** ~ *"She is free to do whatever she wants to make her happy. If fucking other men makes her happy, she can do that. But she can't be with me."*

There isn't some natural design that makes women inherently monogamous. Monogamy isn't in a woman's DNA. The truth is that men are insecure and selfish as fuck, and they created the idea of the virtuous, monogamous woman to appease the uncertainties they have about themselves. The reason why women allow this fallacy to prevail is because men "control" relationships, so they give men the power over their pussies and their relationships out of the need for security.

Initially, I mistakenly believed that Black Men weren't interested in consensual non-monogamy. But the more I probed, the more I realized they don't frown upon the idea of non-monogamy or the Lifestyle at all. In fact, they love it! Most men would love to have multiple partners and would appreciate being with a woman who could accept that kind of relationship. However, it is less common for them to openly ask for these types of relationships because many of them wouldn't be okay with their girlfriends or wives fucking other men. They're fine with attending a play party and dicking down some other man's wife, but the idea of another man fucking theirs is way too much to bear.

Mike, NYC ~ *"I've fucked multiple wives while their husbands watched, and I could tell they weren't always excited about it. Men think because they give good dick, that no one can do it better; not the pussy they fuck regularly. But if they know what I know, ain't nothing like new dick. I don't care how good you're laying it down. So, when I'm giving it to some of these women, I don't think the men are prepared to see or hear how their women respond. I don't think I would be either no matter how much I prepared for it."*

When it comes down to it, it's really the male ego that prevents them from being okay with sharing their women with other men. Some of these men couldn't care less about the fantasies of their women and would prefer not to know about any of them if those fantasies included other men. However, the Lifestyle isn't just about satisfying the pleasures of a man. The choice to Lifestyle should be so that *both* partners can have sexual freedom and find more happiness in their lives together. Just as a woman puts her man's happiness above her insecurities, he must be willing to do the same. A woman's sexual desires are no less important than a man's. Men do understand that but are too ego-driven to admit it. But please don't be misled. Women should have the freedom to express their sexuality however they see fit, not just in ways that are pleasing to a man's ego.

Nou, Tampa ~ *"I love my husband. We have a great relationship, our marriage is great, and we are poly. Occasionally we find women to have sex with and once in a while we may even have a long-term girlfriend. I enjoy women so those situations work when they do. Lately, he and I have been at odds. Sometimes I want to have sex* *with other men but he won't allow it. When I tell him how unfair he's being, he just says he's not comfortable with another man fucking me. "What would that make me if I let another man have what's mine?" is his favorite go-to line. It makes me so upset because it feels like he doesn't care about my happiness. I want him to be as comfortable as I am when he has sex with other women. He says that it isn't the same thing, but to me, it is the same. He likes to watch women strap me up, and that can be fun, but it still isn't what I desire. I wish he could just understand that me having sex with another man, doesn't make him less of a man."*

When women confide in me during coaching sessions or in regular conversation, this is a common theme. These women have desires that are left unfulfilled due to partners who refuse to acknowledge them. When asked what that means for the relationship, most of them say they won't leave their partners even if it means they are unfulfilled. The fear of being alone and having to go through the same issues with another man is enough to make them stay. Several of them admitted to stepping outside of the relationship to get what they need and pray their husbands never find out. I think it's sad that women in non-monogamous relationships have to resort to cheating because their partners are too selfish and insecure to understand that a woman's needs are just as important as theirs.

I have already settled with the idea of never being in a bonded or committed relationship with a man. Once I mention how much I love group sex and getting fucked by two men at the same time, it's curtains. People always ask me if I'm lonely or afraid of dying alone because I reject the monogamous way. My answer will always be no. First and foremost, I don't believe that being in love with another person is the relationship that should be the most meaningful in our lives. The most important relationship any of us should have is the one we have with ourselves. It is impossible to give love to or receive love from any other person if you do not love yourself first.

Secondly, I find that I am happiest when I have the freedom to do whatever it is that makes me happy. I get to decide what's right for me and live life as I see fit. In most relationships, people give up the things that make them the happiest if those things don't align with the goals of the relationship. I no longer wish to do that; I'd much rather be alone. To clarify, being alone or not having a regular or committed partner does not mean I am lonely; I am never lonely. As a solo-polyamorist, I am my primary partner but my range of friends and lovers runs wide. I get what I need when I need it from single individuals and other poly people. I enjoy my own company and have amazing non-sexual friends that I adore who I also enjoy spending time with. As a Black woman in the Lifestyle, I will not compromise how I choose to live just so I can be in a relationship with a man who cares more about his ego than my happiness. Miss me with that bullshit!

Making the Lifestyle choice should be so that both you and your partner can have sexual freedom and find more happiness in your lives together. It shouldn't be a one-way street for either of you to get what you need while leaving your partner unfulfilled and unhappy. The idea is to move away from the restrictions placed upon you by the rules of monogamy and find ways to keep you and your partner fulfilled in as many ways as possible. In the Lifestyle, there are endless pathways to achieving this goal. You just have to be willing to cross the street to see what's on the other side.

LIFESTYLE ETIQUETTE: RULES OF ENTANGLEMENTS

"Having sex with someone isn't a receipt of ownership."

Some people think it's a free for all when they're in a Lifestyle environment. It isn't. A naked woman in a pool is not an invitation for anyone to touch her without permission. Two people fucking in a cabana for others to see does not mean they are looking for others to join. You should never make assumptions about what a person is willing to do with you even if you witness them performing certain acts on someone else. Some men will attempt to join group sex situations, without an invitation, and take offense when they're denied access. Having a dick is not a VIP pass to pussy even when pussy is being offered to others around you. Consent is as important in Lifestyle settings as it is in Vanilla settings. You should never put your hands or any other part of your body on another person unless he/she says that it's okay to do. You should also not assume that someone would be willing to have sex with you just because they happen to be Lifestyle. A lot of men assume that because I enjoy multiples sex or because I'm a nudist, that I would automatically fuck them. This is a grave misconception. I have sex with people who are appealing to me. They meet some standards of mine and having sex with them achieves some goal or fulfills some fantasy. If I am not attracted to you, I will not fuck you, plain and simple. Both men and women take offense when their advances are rejected. I'm not rude but I am pretty clear when I don't desire you. If you're ever rejected, keep it cool and keep it pushing. But also keep in mind that a one-time rejection does not necessarily mean a person never wants to play. It could mean that that moment was not the right time. Additionally, don't take it personally when a person or a couple you've previously played with, rejects your advancements to play a second time. This is a common problem with couples who wish to have more shared experiences with a Unicorn. As a Unicorn myself, I tend to have this issue, especially with older couples who may be looking for someone to join them regularly.

I played with a married couple one afternoon at an LS event. I wasn't super attracted to the wife, but the husband was very sexy, tall, and well built. The wife's body wasn't to my liking, but she had good energy and I could tell she really wanted me for her husband. When she said her husband wanted to fuck me, we exited the pool without hesitation to have a quick session in my room. It was a bit rushed but I learned the hard way to never delay a potentially good fuck session. In the LS people like to quickly plan and coordinate sex but then change their minds just as fast.

Once in my room, the three of us hopped in the shower. She immediately dropped to her knees to lick my pussy while her husband sucked my nipples. He grabbed me by the throat and jammed his tongue into my mouth. They were both rather tall which made me feel vulnerable and tame. I like that feeling when I'm with couples because usually, I'm the aggressive beast. When she stood up, I dropped to my knees and gobbled up his dick. He was thick and long and became erect immediately once inside my mouth. I sucked him aggressively ensuring that the juiciness in my mouth made a frothy mess. While still on my knees, I gripped his dick with one hand, turned to her, and slid my tongue between her lips. She let out a loud guttural moan that enticed me to slide my fingers inside her. Suddenly, the husband scooped me up, exited the shower, and threw me onto the bed. He spread my legs, pulled them back, and jammed his tongue inside my ass. As he licked me, she laid down beside me, kissed my breasts and my lips then softly pulled my hair back from my face. While we kissed, her husband put on a condom, pushed my legs back again, and slid his thick dick inside my warm, pink pussy. I growled as he entered me, and I immediately matched the rhythm of his strokes. He was shocked at how easily I managed his size and the weight of his body pressed into mine. He grabbed the back of my thighs, raised his hips, and dug in as deep as he could go. She continued to kiss me and rub on my clit as he pounded away at my insides. As I started to cum, I commanded him not to stop, letting him know I was about to explode and stopping short of that would be unbecoming. When I exploded, my pussy pulsated with every quickened thrust, and shortly thereafter, he busted his nut, howling like a beast in the night. She sat up quickly to lick the juices oozing from my pussy and as he pulled off the condom, she leaned in and sucked the cum from his dick. It was a high sex energy session that I really enjoyed, but once it was over, we showered and returned to the pool area.

The days following, more people arrived, and I set my sights on fucking other couples. When I saw the couple throughout the day, I would casually speak, but sometimes I would catch the husband watching me as I entertained other people. He didn't look too pleased with me, but I didn't care. I rarely let other people's emotions stop my fun. Eventually, their energy toward me changed and they no longer spoke to me. I'd say hello, and the wife would give me a half-smile, but the husband would just roll his eyes and look away. I knew that somehow, they felt slighted either by my behavior toward others or the fact that I had no interest in revisiting sexual contact with them. For the remainder of their stay, they never spoke to me again.

I almost wanted to laugh while writing this because of how petty the husband behaved. I couldn't believe that both of them would be upset about my not wanting to have sex with them again to the point of not speaking to me. FYI: having sex with someone isn't a receipt of ownership. You don't earn the right to play with someone on Friday simply because you had sex with them on Tuesday. You fucked, it was fun, now move on. Catching feelings in those environments is not wise and being rude to people because they don't want you is unappealing and immature.

There is a level of respect that must be appreciated in any LS environment. Just as there are guidelines that govern any club or organization, there is a particular Lifestyle etiquette that is practiced among its participants. As you and your partner begin venturing out and attending different LS clubs, parties, and events, you will become more comfortable with the flow of things. Although specific codes of behavior can be drastically different from person to person, and relationship to relationship, it's important for you to understand basic Lifestyle principles that will keep you safe, respectable, and desirable.

* **Check your emotions at the door.** This was last, but after recent events, I felt compelled to make it top priority. Do not come to LS environments expecting to fall in love, find your soulmate, or meet the one. I'm not saying that it *can't* happen. But I would be remiss if I didn't caution you about keeping your emotions in check. Although it may be tempting, and you may feel better

than you ever have in your life, do not get emotionally caught up in the people or the experiences in these environments. Most of the people you will meet are looking to have a great fucking time. When you share yourself with "good time" people, enjoy the moments and search for the next. The individuals or couples that are looking for more will let you know they want more. Don't be pushy, overly aggressive, or clingy. You must learn how to have amazing experiences and leave them right where you found them.

* **Don't touch without permission.** Often, nudity or bare minimum clothing is involved at LS events. Although you and your partner may be tempted to touch a cute ass walking by, make sure you have consent before you touch. Nudity is not consent. Likewise, don't accept being touched by others without your consent. People tend to get touchy-feely, especially when alcohol and drugs are involved. If you ever feel uncomfortable in a particular space, remove yourself or ask the offender to move on. Don't be afraid to escalate the situation if needed. Too many times, I've gone to LS events where some of the men think they can touch on titties and asses just because they're exposed.

* **Don't assume a woman is alone or single even if she appears to be by herself.** On the other hand, if a man and a woman arrive together or are together, assume they are in a relationship until you confirm otherwise. Some people think it›s a sign of disrespect not to acknowledge their partner. If you're interested in a particular woman or man, simply ask if the person is with anyone. Some couples choose to socialize separately for their own reasons. If one of them is an introvert, it makes sense that the extroverted partner would likely be seen alone more often. Once

you get confirmation that the person is solo, you have a green light to carry on. You want to avoid looking like a poacher as must as possible, so play it safe, and ask questions.

* **Be honest about your relationship status.** Whether you›re married, single, in a relationship, or an entanglement, just be honest. Many married LS couples choose to only engage in sex with other married couples. Even when it's just the wives having sex, some couples prefer to only engage in sex with people who are making equal compromises and therefore prefer to deal with couples who are equally yoked. If you and your partner are in a relationship, but unmarried, that situation may be more tolerable than if you were single and just fucking. Contrary to that, some couples prefer only single women. If a woman is single but is with an FWB (friend with benefits), they usually have an understanding about how to engage when someone wants to fuck only one of them. If she's cleared to party with whomever she chooses, you wouldn't need to be concerned about the male friend at all. Alternatively, if a full swap couple wants to fuck you and your FWB, although you are "together" for the purpose of attendance, some husbands may want to know if he's giving consent for a single man to fuck his wife. You should never lie about who you are or what it is you want. If you and your partner are just FWBs, be honest and say that. Misrepresenting yourself is super immature, distasteful, and will ruin your reputation and your prospects in the Lifestyle community.

* **Maintain communication with the partner of the same gender unless you get the okay to do otherwise.** Here›s the thing, so many women have trust issues, more specifically, trusting other women with their men. So, if you're interested in a couple as

potential playmates, things tend to be easier when the women have established a connection. As a personal rule, I don't engage with the male of a couple more than the female. My preference is to create a bond with her, and once there's a vibe, I become more comfortable engaging with her man. When the female isn't engaged much at all, I take that as a sign that she isn't interested, and I move on. I do not deal with couples when the female partner has a bad attitude, an ugly disposition, or seems disinterested in me. So please, please, please, be polite, friendly, and welcoming.

Men tend to prefer maintaining communication with the male partner when dealing with couples as well. For the same reasons as a woman, it is better when the partners of the same gender build a bond unless otherwise agreed upon. It helps ease the doubt that may be ruminating in a partner's mind when same-gender bonds are formed. That said, if you're unhappy for any reason, or you and your partner aren't in a good space, don't show up to a social event dragging your negative energy with you. Keep your ass at home. If you are the type of person that tends to feel intimidated by the presence of other attractive people, you must learn how to set your insecurities aside. It doesn't make sense to show up to an event, then have an attitude the entire time. Work on yourself so that you can be a better swingman for your partner.

* **Ensure you and your partner are on the same page.** Be very clear about your preferences, what you're looking for, and what both of you are comfortable doing. This includes ensuring your energies are aligned and handling any beefs you may have between you. When the two of you aren't on the same page, all sorts of problems can arise. I've witnessed couples arguing and

fighting in private settings and at public events. I'm amazed at some of the behavior people aren't embarrassed to display when others are present. Again, if the two of you are having problems, the last place you should be is in an environment where you can easily be distracted by other people and piss your partner off even more. Keep your personal problems to yourselves and work them out at home before inviting other people into your spcae.

* **Always check in with your partner.** This is a must. Create a safe word, a signal, or anything that you and your partner can agree on that once it's seen or heard, both of you know it's time to go have a talk. A check-in should happen before agreeing to play or wandering off with others, during sex play, and after playing to ensure that all is well. Something as simple as a head nod could be enough to alert your partner to the need to converse or indicate that everything is okay. Whatever you choose, it should be something the two of you can easily understand. Here are four key things to remember while at an LS event:

1. Never walk off with people, whether you know them or not, without informing your partner. Unless you and your partner have a clear understanding that either of you are free to roam without checking in, just give your partner a quick heads up before taking off. (It's common courtesy, and it stops the search party before it happens. Trust me, it happens.)

2. If you're consenting to sex that includes your partner, make sure he/she knows about it beforehand. You may want to fuck someone your partner may never be attracted to and if

you agree to playtime without your partner's knowledge, it could be a disaster. So just ask.

3. During a sexual encounter, make eye contact, give a thumbs up, stick out your tongue, anything to signify your comfort or the lack thereof. I've been saved from many bad encounters with a quick shake of the head. Sometimes you don't know a situation is undesirable until you're butt naked and about to get busy. Then you get a whiff of a rancid body odor that makes you want to puke. Something as easy as a sneeze could alert your partner that it's time to abort mission.

4. Always confirm that all went well and there's little need for concern afterward. You can have a conversation as soon as it's over or wait until bedtime. It all depends on what makes you comfortable. The reason for this is to make sure that both of you are okay especially if you end up having sex in separate locations. If you ever feel threatened or if someone did anything to disrespect you, it's important to let your partner know. Some men have the tendency to get overly aggressive with women they view as another man's property. They may even get slick and remove their condoms when they think a woman is unaware. These men must be exposed. They should not be allowed to roam freely through these environments without everyone knowing what happened. So never be afraid to disclose events that left you feeling hurt, threatened, or disrespected.

*   **Hygiene! Hygiene! Hygiene!** Did I say hygiene? Good hygiene is non-negotiable. Be cognizant of the environment and how your body responds to it. If you know that you get funky or tart down

there after a few hours of dancing or fun in the sun, make sure you have the supplies you need to freshen up as often as you need to. It's common courtesy, really, and it shows you care about yourself and creating a great experience for others you interact with. You would think this was a given. But I promise you, it is not. You must know your own body. Don't just assume you smell okay. *"I want to smell your funky pussy or your stinky balls,"* says no one. It takes a second to discover you need to clean up a bit. I must also address the importance of fresh breath. First of all, if you have bad breath daily, you probably need to visit your dentist and orthodontist. But if you've been eating seafood, onions, garlic, or you're the type whose breath smells when you're drinking, please bring a toothbrush, toothpaste, or gum with you. I typically carry what I refer to as my "Shag Bag" wherever I go. Inside I have all of the essentials to ensure I'm always ready for a good time.

Shag Bag contents from head to toe:
- ✓ Eye drops
- ✓ Toothbrush/paste, mouthwash, mints, floss
- ✓ Deodorant
- ✓ Lip gloss, chapstick
- ✓ Cleansing wipes (for pits, asses, puss, and cocks)
- ✓ Condoms (L/XL)
- ✓ Body spray and lotion
- ✓ Lube (water-based & nori seaweed)

Make a Shag Bag and keep it stocked and handy at all times. It may save you from the most embarrassing moments of your life.

* **Always bring your own condoms.** It's a shame that this has to be stressed but you would be surprised at the number of men who don't bring their own condoms knowing full well sex is going to happen. Ladies, it is not just a man's responsibility to bring protection. I ALWAYS have my own condoms. ALWAYS. Make sure you have different sizes and brands if you want to cover your bases. Just bring your own. Never rely on the availability of condoms no matter where you go. You're too mature to miss out on opportunities because you don't have protection.

PLAYMATES & PLAYDATES

"Unicorns value their freedom...
They're there for a good time, not a long time."

Finding compatible singles and couples to play with can be very challenging. Searching through the mud to find the diamonds is the best way to describe how difficult it can be to navigate through the prospects to find suitable playmates. There are so many things to consider: ethnicity, height and weight, single or married, soft vs. full swap, whether a person or couple just wants sex or looking for long-term bonds, and what someone's individual kinks may be. You will obviously have preferences, but understand that what you prefer may not always be available, and the higher your standards are, the lower your play pool will be.

Whether I'm paired up with an FWB or on my Unicorn flow, my preference is always very attractive, fit, Black and Brown, couples or singles. As a Black woman who prefers Black partners, my options are oftentimes limited at big events considering we rarely make an appearance, so, unfortunately, that isn't what I always end up with. Now don't get it twisted, although my preferences are of the browner persuasions, if a person of a different ethnicity is fuckable, then I will fuck. I also prefer partners who have athletic builds with limited excess fat. I am a highly active and energetic woman and prefer partners that have the stamina and endurance to please me adequately. These are all characteristics that I prefer and look for in potential playmates, but if I walked into every Lifestyle environment only willing to fuck those types, I would be assed out a lot. Most LS environments are not exclusive and are pretty diverse in terms of body type, age, and relationship style, and not always to my liking. So often, I have to make small compromises to achieve my goal to fuck at that particular moment. The point is to get as close to what you prefer to fulfill your needs in any situation. Therefore, if your goal is to find people to have sex with, but none meet your specific requirements, you have to be willing to make compromises when necessary. Things are even trickier when you're a couple, so you must establish your plan of attack.

* Who do you want to play with? Is it couples or singles?

* Will you seek partners together or go solo and bring prospects back to your partner?

* Who will take the lead in initiating contact? Will both partners be allowed to make advancements equally, or does either partner prefer to do the choosing because he/she has better taste?

* What are you willing to compromise should you find mismatched couples? Is either of you willing to take one for the team? If so, whose turn is it?

These are some of the things to consider as you look for prospective playmates. When a couple moves as a unit, they typically have clear objectives and work towards achieving their goals. Keep in mind that the people you choose may not want to play with you, as they also have their objectives that may not align with yours. You must also be able to accept rejection, which is very common in LS environments. Having an attitude or becoming disrespectful simply because someone said no, is immature and unacceptable. Understand, no matter how attractive you think you are or how confident you may be in your abilities to please others sexually, you may not be everyone's cup of tea. Also, it's important to keep in mind that when you are with a partner, there isn't one, but two people that another person or couple has to find fuckable. So, when you roll with a less than desirable partner, it will have a bearing on your level of success in those environments.

Unicorns

Unicorns are probably the easiest playmates to find. There are always single women at LS events of all shapes, sizes, and ethnicities, willing to play to some degree. But Unicorns are special because they are bi-sexual and interested in sex with couples as well. Single women who hang out in those spaces typically understand that they are a commodity and find other singles or couples to play with. Not all Unicorns are created equally. Therefore, you have to know what you want and be clear about your expectations when seeking one out. Some are in the LS solely for the sex, and there isn't anything wrong with that. However, if you and your partner are looking for a serious girlfriend, at some point, this should be discussed with the Unicorn you are pursuing.

Unicorns value their freedom. When you hook up with one, don't attempt to lay claim to her because you had a good time. She doesn't belong to you, she isn't yours for the night unless she agrees to that, and she isn't obligated to revisit a turn with you. Just enjoy the experience, stash it in your memory bank, and move on. She's there for a good time, not a long time. So many couples have a hard time understanding this basic concept, especially when they get with a Unicorn that's highly desirable and fucks them well. There's nothing worse than a couple catching feelings when they see a Unicorn they fucked, enjoying other people afterward. Check your feelings, don't take it personally, and find someone else.

When seeking playmates, the most important thing is that both of you are on the same page and have an understanding of what you're looking for. You will run into some challenges if you don't have similar tastes in women. Some men will choose to fuck a woman because she has a fat ass, even if she's not that attractive. As for women, if you are anything like me and you're intrigued by aesthetics, this simply would not do. For me to be interested, a woman has to be attractive. A fat ass is a bonus, but not a necessity. Men have a hard time getting that. *"I'm not fucking her face"* is their go-to line. However, when a woman is sucking my pussy, and I look down at her face, I don't want someone I'm not attracted to looking up at me. It's just that simple. Know your partner and the kind of women he/she is attracted to. If the two of you can't agree on someone, one of you may have to bow out and let the other handle that alone.

Couples

Finding compatible couples to play with is a bit more complicated. Looking for one fuckable person is difficult enough, but trying to get two that come as a package deal, is definitely more challenging, but not impossible. Oftentimes couples are "mismatched" meaning one of them is attractive and the other not so much. I›m sure you›ve seen couples together and wondered, "Why is she with him?" Well, you'll be thinking it a lot more as you navigate through Lifestyle environments. However, the "why" isn't important. The important thing is, are they fuckable? You will encounter a variety of couple combinations that will cause you to ponder whether you would or wouldn't have sex. Keep in mind that everyone isn't attracted to the same kind of person and the people in these environments come in all shapes and sizes. The preferences of you and your partner are the only ones you should be concerned about but oftentimes you need a little math to help make your decision. That is when the Scale of Fuckability comes in handy.

I like to use The Scale of Fuckability (SOF) when choosing my playmates, especially in environments where there are limited opportunities to get to know people before sexual interactions occur. The SOF is based on appearance and sex appeal in your eyes and is a quick way to determine if having sex would be beneficial to you and your partner. Oftentimes decisions to have sex must be made rather swiftly and it helps to have your minimum SOF range. The scale starts at ten ends at zero, and both partners are scored as a unit or team. Here are examples of the scoring system:

20 – Woman is hot (10) + Man is hot (10) (Highly fuckable)

16 - Woman is hot (9) + Man is mediocre (7) (If she's highly fuckable, she could trump what he lacks as long as he isn't unfuckable)

14 - Woman (7) + Man (7) are mediocre (Somewhat fuckable as long as neither is unfuckable. Sex appeal and the size of the packages can help play up other qualities they may lack)

13 - Man is good (8) + Woman is not (5 or less) (Less than fuckable. The woman is usually the main draw, so if she is unfuckable, it probably wouldn't be worth it)

10 - Man (5) + Woman (5) are not. (Unfuckable)

This scale is solely based on outward appearance. It does not factor in personality or social disposition. It should not be used to determine whether or not a person would make a good mate. It is predominantly used for the purpose of establishing the likelihood of sex to occur with an individual or a couple. Obviously, you would want both partners to be hot, but often this is not the case. As superficial as it may be, I have found it to be very helpful in LS environments. Unlike in the Vanilla world, where you have the chance to get to know people through conversations and lunch dates, there is very limited time to make any other impression besides a physical one. Time is of the essence, especially if you're interested in a highly fuckable couple. Everybody wants to fuck them, so you have to get in where you fit in and make your intentions known. Lifestyle environments are highly erogenous atmospheres where things move at a fast pace. The longer you take to make a move on a couple you may be interested in, the greater the chances are that someone else will swoop in and catch their attention. You don't want to miss out on your opportunity to make a connection because you needed to do a personality check first.

Once you establish fuckability, you need to address the rules in which couples operate under. No two couples have the same agreements as to what is acceptable during sex. Even amongst couples who are full swap, an act such as anal penetration of the wife by another man may be off-limits. Sometimes nothing is off-limits, but it is important to establish that before any type of play begins, or someone is bound to catch feelings.

We loved to fuck while people watched. We chose an open area draped with sheer red curtains, which made it easy for the voyeurs to observe and join. While I was on my knees sucking my man's dick, a pretty little Brown thing approached us and asked if she could taste me. I looked her over while I continued to suck and established she was highly fuckable. I unwrapped my mouth from around him, and she kneeled down beside me. As he stepped back to give us space to enjoy one another, she pushed me down on the floor and spread my legs. "May I?" she asked, talking to me but looking over at a man I assumed was hers. He was also fuckable, with a nice build and thick dick. I remember thinking, "Finally! A sexy couple we can get down with." As she slid down between my thighs, she started to softly lick my pussy with her wet, warm tongue. I moaned and leaned into her mouth, and as I did, she slid two fingers inside me. The faster she licked, the more I desired to taste her. When she came up for air, I flipped her onto her back and took my turn. As I licked and sucked her sweet flesh, she tried to squirm away, reaching her hand out to her man for approval. He just sat there, watching, as did mine from across the room. Both she and I were sexually aggressive and took turns flipping each other to lick and suck one another everywhere. More people started to gather to watch our glistening bodies entangled beneath the red lights, kissing and licking one another. I was stronger than she was, so once I got her onto her back again, she couldn't release herself from me. I had one goal in mind, which was to make her cum hard while everyone watched. I licked her pussy from top to bottom while applying pressure to her inner walls with my fingers. As her moans grew louder and she started to cum, my man couldn't stand by and watch any longer. He came up behind me and tried to slide inside me. But as he took hold of my hips, her man came across the room and grabbed his arm. I couldn't tell what was happening behind me, but later he told me that her man didn't want him to join us. He only wanted to watch his woman receive pleasure from another woman. That was their boundary; woman on woman only with no male interaction. The only problem was that her man couldn't stop mine from doing what he wanted with me. He was turned on and wanted to dig inside me while I was face deep between her thighs. My man wasn't trying to touch the other woman but her man needed to make known what was permissible. They exchanged words, and before long, my man slid up inside me, fucking me hard, while I continued to suck *the juice from her pussy. Her man stood close by, standing guard to ensure my man didn't violate his terms. Once she was finished cumming, she slid from beneath me, and they walked away.*

This was one of those situations where things got tricky because we began to play without exchanging words to discuss specific limitations. They were a soft swap couple that didn't allow contact between the female and another man. Obviously, we didn't know that because she joined us without saying she *only* wanted me. My man would have definitely tried to have his way with her until her man intervened. Things could have gone extremely bad if either of the men were really hot-headed and unable to control heightened emotions. Again, this is why it's important to state your needs, especially when you have specific boundaries and you're approaching people already having sex. It's difficult to determine what a person or couple is into if words aren't spoken.

Full swap couples tend to be a bit more easy-going in terms of what is or isn't acceptable. Typically, all parties are interested in ensuring the needs of their partners are fulfilled. In full swap situations such as MFFM, the women have sex with each other and both males. These scenarios tend to work out pretty well as long as everyone is on the same page. When the couples are both highly fuckable, the sex energy that is created is intense. Sometimes things don't always go as planned, so you must be willing to make adjustments when needed.

One of my FWBs invited me out to a Lifestyle social club with him and his friends. I had never met this couple before, but they were an attractive bi-racial couple that were also Lifestylers. The club was uneventful. There was no one there we wanted to fuck besides ourselves, so we took our little party home. All of us had way too much to drink, but we decided to play anyway. The female partner of the couple was White and hot as fuck. She was really pretty, with nice breasts and wide hips. She and I had really good sex energy, and I couldn't wait to find out what she tasted like. As we all undressed, I immediately went for her and dropped to my knees to lick between her thighs. She was still standing but lost her balance as I worked her pussy out with my tongue. As she laid back on the sofa, my friend slid his dick into her mouth. Her man slid underneath me and started to suck my pussy from below. After I got my fill, I sat up to suck my friend's dick. She slid off the sofa and started to do the same to her man. For whatever reason, her man was having difficulty getting hard. It was late, we had way too much to drink, and we were all tired. I got on my knees and my friend started to fuck me. Her man then slid his dick into my mouth to see if he would have a different response. He didn't. The more frustrated he got, the more he killed the vibe, so eventually, we all stopped, found a place to sleep, and passed out.

Early the next morning, I woke up hot and bothered. My friend was asleep beside me, but I never let that stop me from getting what I want in the morning. I started to suck his dick until he awakened. Once he was awake, I slid a condom on, climbed on top, and we started to fuck. Her man was downstairs but heard us fucking and came upstairs. He quickly slid his dick into my mouth while I rode my friend. This time, her man had no issue getting hard and wanted to try me out. Instead of dismounting one dick, I told the other to join us and penetrate me anally. He slid on a condom, poured the lube into my ass, then slowly slid inside me. The three of us continued to fuck like that for some time, with me sandwiched between them, both holes full and throbbing. The one in the back couldn't hold out any longer and was the first to cum. I was close to cumming, and his orgasm brought me closer to finishing. After he removed himself, my friend flipped me over to finish me off. As he pounded me face down ass up, both of us came hard and loud. In that moment, I realized that she never came up to join us. I love to cum with women, so her presence was missed. Once we were done, we went to shower, and there she was, laying on her bed grinning at me. When I asked her why she didn't join us, she simply said she had them plenty and wanted me to enjoy myself.

Full swap couples are the best. They're typically in tune with one another and are truly interested in ensuring their partners receive the pleasure they deserve. Although that time the other female didn't fully participate, she gave her man the space to get what he desired, which was to have me. The four of us are now good friends and will hang out and fuck from time to time, bringing in extra bodies to keep it exciting. More often than not, friendships are created from these entanglements. When you find people who are like-minded, sexual, freaky, and interested in having a good time, it's likely to happen.

That said, finding playmates that you can connect with and fuck from time to time may not be your only objective. If you're interested in more than just sex, you have much more to consider when seeking playmates. Fuckability may not be as high on your compatibility list because you're also looking to build friendships or relationships. In which case, taking your time to get to know a Unicorn or a couple is important.

While in my open relationship, we sought out attractive, sexually uninhibited people with whom we could hang out, travel with, and fuck. We desired to be free, to do as we pleased wherever we were, and it was more comfortable to do so in the presence of like-minded people. We met several couples during our year together, but most of them conducted their relationships very differently than ours, so it was never really a good fit. Most of them wanted to date and bond before having sex. But we were very impatient, and when others weren't as open as we were or needed time for a friendship to develop before sex occurred, we shut them down. It was sex or nothing for us, and that probably gave them pause.

If you're looking to make real connections with other people, understand that it takes time and patience to build relationships when multiple people are involved. I've been in the Lifestyle as a Unicorn longer than I was a part of a couple, so I understand how couples roll from both perspectives. Looking back, I think perhaps he and I were too aggressive in our efforts and not understanding enough of other people's needs. Because of that, we never established friendships or found a core group of playmates both of us could enjoy.

Initiating Contact

As a couple, you must establish who will seek out potential playmates for both of you. In some relationships, either the male or female partner can look for and make advances to individuals they see as good prospects. This means that either partner can initiate contact with others, then set up a time and space for introductions. This works when both partners are confident in each other's ability to find acceptable playmates. In other relationships, the authority to find prospects is given to only one partner. The choice to have one designated person to find hook-ups may be related to trust issues, lack of time, or because one of them has better taste, and his/her judgment is trusted by the other partner. More often than not, I've found that the female partner usually takes the lead, especially when seeking female playmates, because women tend to be more particular about whose pussy they are willing to lick.

> **Chris, Miami** ~ *"I usually let my wife choose the women we sleep with. She never likes my choices. She always finds something wrong with the girl. I'm not that picky. I just want to fuck. She worries about the girl's hair, her clothes, even the sound of her voice. I don't know what any of that has to do with fucking, but I don't waste my time anymore. All I want is a female that looks good and has good hygiene. As long as I get that, I'm game. So, I just play the back and let her do her thing because if she doesn't like the girl, nothing is going to happen anyway. I want her to find women she likes because it makes it better for me in the end."*

This arrangement works well because the husband would rather defer to his wife than waste his time trying to find female playmates his wife may like. With the wife taking the lead, she ensures that the women coming into her bed are ones that she has a greater chance of enjoying. She also ensures that women who may have other agendas have little opportunity to infiltrate the relationship and create chaos.

Tiffany, LA ~ *"My husband and I found a woman we were both excited to play with. She was very sexy and came on to me hard. I'm really into women and actually looking for a girlfriend for us, so I love getting with one that really enjoys being with women. The first few times we played, she was all over me, and the three of us had a great time. We took her on a few vacations with us, and she seemed to be a good fit. But soon, she started to contact my husband instead of me for things she wanted, and they developed a relationship that didn't include me. She once called him and asked him for money, which I did not appreciate at all. When I told her as much, she acted as if she hadn't done anything wrong. After all, "he was her man too." I felt like it was disrespectful, but my husband wasn't too bothered, although he didn't give her the money. As time went on, the two of them got closer, but she and I rarely interacted. She stopped calling me, and when they would get together, I wasn't invited. I told him I wasn't a fan of the relationship, and I felt like her agenda the entire time was to be with him, without my involvement. His judgment was clouded at that time because he developed feelings for her, and he thought I was just being insecure. But eventually, she showed her true colors when she started to tell him that he didn't need me, that they could have a better relationship than the one we had. It was at that point that he felt she crossed the line and ended the relationship. I believe she was a fake from the start and wasn't really into women at all. She pretended to want me, but what she really wanted was to plot on my man so that she could have my life. It's a shame that bitches still be plotting even when you give them the green light to fuck."*

It took Tiffany's husband a while to see what she saw from the time the other woman stopped communicating with her but maintained contact with him. Once Tiffany felt like the other woman was overstepping, she and her husband should have had a serious conversation about the other relationship. Tiffany's concerns were valid and she was right to bring them to his attention. Her husband needed to give more time to his wife to consider her concerns, instead of minimizing her feelings. He felt like she was being insecure and wanted to end the relationship because she was jealous. However, Tiffany didn't like how the other woman moved and felt as if she had a different agenda than what they originally discussed. Tiffany did not have veto power so she couldn't force her husband to end the relationship, nor did she want to. She wanted him to figure things out himself, which he did eventually. The need for this conversation should have fallen under their agreement to discuss any matters of concern if they established such an agreement.

A woman should definitely be leery of playmates who try hard to connect with her man, but have little interest in her, especially if the original relationship was between the three of them. Unfortunately, this can happen, which gives many women pause when it comes to sharing their men. If the two of you meet a woman together, and she starts as a playmate for both of you but then stops communicating with you while still trying to fuck your man, her ass is up to something. If your agreement is that he can have relationships with other women that don't involve you, then it's up to him to curb behaviors that could be detrimental to his primary relationship. Situations like this occur when a couple isn›t on the same page regarding acceptable behavior as it relates to other partners. If the two of you don›t see eye to eye, it will not be difficult for others to infiltrate or disrupt your relationship. This is why some couples maintain a particular communication method that helps keep the drama to a minimum.

When it comes to partners looking for other couples to play with, the plan of attack is usually somewhat different. In some relationships, they prefer to keep same-gender communication only, i.e., the women only reach out to each other, not the men, or they communicate together as a group, such as in a group chat on a social media platform. This helps to keep the lines of communication open and safe and minimizes the chances of potential indiscretions between parties. From my experience, things work out better when there is same-gender communication or everyone communicates as a group. It's easier to determine the level of interest of all parties involved when the conversations occur simultaneously. It also helps everyone feel more secure when they are aware of their partners' communications with others. When and if connections are formed amongst the group, it's up to the people involved to determine what type of communication is comfortable for them.

Generally, when I am interested in a couple, I prefer to converse with just the female partner or speak to both partners jointly in a group chat. I prefer not to have conversations with the male partner that don't involve the female. This way, I am able to bond with her woman-to-woman, and it helps to minimize any anxiety she may feel about me fucking her man. Some women just want to be reassured that other women aren't trying to fuck their men and run off with them. Once we become friends and a level of comfort is established between each of us, I may communicate with either partner at any given time because the relationship has grown into that.

Compromising

Taking one for the team is not something that any partner wants to do when it comes to finding playmates. However, it may be necessary on some occasions. Taking one for the team means that somebody will win, but the other partner is somehow taking a loss. This is a common issue when you're in an LS environment, where your choices are minimal, and you tend to have higher standards. Sometimes a couple may see a woman they both want to fuck, but the man she's with is less than desirable. If they want to full swap, the female partner may choose to bite the bullet and play with the less desirable man just to get the woman she and her partner desire. This isn't always necessary as the female partner could refuse the other man. However, some couples will not allow penetration of their partner if the other couple isn't willing to reciprocate the offer. Relationships are about making compromises, and those who engage in non-monogamous sex and relationships are no exception.

When choosing couples as playmates, finding ones whom you have a 100% connection with is rare. They are out there, but it's less common to find a couple where the male and female are 100% compatible with you and yours. There's bound to be a mismatch somewhere in a four-way, so you have to decide if the mismatch is enough to trump what could potentially be a really good time.

I know that I've taken one for the team on more than one occasion because of my partner's desire to be with other women when I wasn't in the mood for it, or I wasn't really into the women in general. He in turn, also did so when I had the desire to fuck him alone with other men, which was not his favorite thing to do. It's a judgment call that you will have to make, not under coercion or duress, but simply because you want to keep your partner satisfied.

Mai, D.C. ~ *"My husband doesn't really want me to fuck other men. It's not something he can settle his mind around. The only way I can really do it is if he's fucking another woman at the same time or if he's just not involved at all. Sometimes, when we're out looking for partners, he may see a woman he likes that I'm not interested in. But I'll agree to have sex with her because I know at some point I'll* *want another man, and I need him to be okay with that happening. We are making compromises so that both of us are happy in the relationship."*

Compromising for the sake of your partner is necessary at times, but it obviously isn't optimal. No one should be taking one for the team every single time you find partners to have sex with. If you find that it's a common problem, you're probably looking for sex in the wrong places. As you seek out partners, be mindful that what may be presented to you for sex in those environments may not be the same as what you would typically look for in a man or woman when you want more than just sex. Your playmates do not have to be people who you would lust over constantly. They can be various sizes and levels of attractiveness, so don't be quick to throw away the barrel because of a few bad apples in it. Sometimes, sex energy can trump attractiveness. If an orgy situation is about to jump off with a couple of 6's on the scale of fuckability, but they are ready to get down with whatever, although aesthetically you know you could do better, a quick thirty-minute trip to the playroom with two 6's could be better than the night ending with zero.

FINAL THOUGHTS

"You have nothing and are nothing without honesty."

Considering what we already know about this society, it is highly unlikely that it will ever openly embrace Lifestyle culture. Monogamy is not just a social construct for relationships. Monogamy is a business, marriage is a transaction, and divorce is the termination of a contract. All of that makes money. Did you know that on the global market, wedding services are worth $300 billion annually?[7] That's just the wedding. That doesn't include the bridal shower, the bachelor and bachelorette party, the honeymoon, or the other big one: *divorce*.

What does divorce look like in numbers? Check this out. According to the World Population Review[8], about 50% of married couples in the United States get divorced. That is the sixth highest divorce rate in the world. Subsequent marriages have an even higher divorce rate: 60% of second marriages end in divorce, and 73% of all third marriages end in divorce. The divorce industry is worth $50 billion per year. Ain't no way in hell this society will ever normalize behavior that is not aligned with the monogamous marriage construct. There is simply too much money at stake to make non-monogamy the new normal. Normalizing the Lifestyle would destroy core Christian values and obliterate the very fabric of the institutions that benefit from the monogamous lie. This society doesn't care if you're happily married. As long as you continue to bankroll the ideology of monogamous love, they will continue to sell the fantasy to you.

Believe it or not, most people, men, in particular, do not believe in monogamy. We have been conditioned for centuries to believe that true love is for one person and those of us who challenge that idea are immoral. But the more I research and continue to have these discussions amongst people from all walks of life, I realize that most people believe that monogamy is a charade. It is something folks do in the public eye, to appear normal and to avoid scrutiny. But in their hearts and behind closed doors they desire to be freed from the restrictive ways and unrealistic expectations of monogamy.

If you've read this far, you're probably questioning whether or not monogamy is for you. Regardless of race or ethnicity, we need to step out of the shadows and start having the kinds of relationships that make us happy. People of color particularly need to embrace all that Lifestyle culture has to offer. This way of life is not just for White people, and those that think that way really need to let go of that ignorant and negative thought pattern. White people don't label it their shit; we do. We have the capability to do all the things in life we wish to do. We simply have to do them.

If you're waiting for nudity, threesomes, and cuckolding to become normalized behavior, you'll die waiting. We must stop placing limitations on ourselves out of fear of what others may say, not realizing that people will talk shit about us no matter what we do. Let them talk, and while they talk, we will live.

You only have one life to live, so live it. Stop letting society tell you how to love or be loved, how to fuck or get fucked. Stop hiding who you are sexually and emotionally just to fit in a box labeled "normal." Normal is boring as fuck! So, if you want your life to be different, then you have to do different shit. Aren't you ready to open up your mind to try something different and exciting? Or are you going to continue on the merry-go-round, in and out of monogamous relationships hoping you will find that "one" person to be happy with forever?

I challenge you to sit your lover down and express your deepest sexual fantasies. Don't hide them; release them! Find out what gets his dick hard and your pussy wet. Everyone has desires they are ashamed to reveal, even to those they've been with for many years. Maybe you'll discover you have quite a few kinks in common. Perhaps you'll realize you don't know your partner much at all. I promise you, if you've never had these conversations, you are in for a surprise. I realize these aren't the easiest conversations to have, but every person in or entering into a relationship should have them. To be in a space where two people break the emotional chains and expose themselves takes courage and a secure emotional aptitude that is lost on so many. Being honest about what really turns you on, the things you think about when you're fucking your partner or even when you masturbate, will not be easy things for your partner to hear, especially if these thoughts involve other people, but the truth should be spoken. Create a safe, non-judgmental space to have these conversations, so your partner is able to receive those truths with an open mind.

Non-monogamy is not for everyone; nothing ever is. For those of you who are convinced that monogamy is the only way and are satisfied with the relationships you have, that's great! Carry on. But for the rest of you who are pretending that monogamy is life, but out here in these streets with two and three other lovers, meanwhile, you have a whole bae at home, need to stop lying to yourselves. You're already non-monogamous, except you're a liar and a cheater because your partner doesn't know it yet. You have the ability to change that narrative if you could only set your fears and insecurities aside.

If you're afraid to live your truth and continue to allow your insecurities to control your life, you will never achieve sexual freedom. The idea that love somehow diminishes when someone you love fucks another is a big ass lie. Sex is not love- never has been and never will be. That entire narrative was created to control who and how you fuck. As long as you continue to equate love with that explosion in your brain when you cum, you'll never be able to tolerate your partner fucking someone else. However, once you're able to separate sex from love, you *will* be able to tap into your own desires and be your true self.

You have to start somewhere. Once you've settled on trying non-monogamy, there are several key things that must be in place before letting other people into your bed.

1. The first thing is a good foundation. Your relationship must be secure. If you're carrying around old baggage from past hurts, already dealing with insecurity and jealousy, or have poor communication, this is not the time to get involved with this Lifestyle. You must take care of home first. Get a relationship coach, seek therapy for yourself and your partner and work through your issues. Your relationship must be intact before attempting to transform what you have into something new.

2. The second thing is trust. Your relationship is nothing without trust. Trusting your partner is critical to the success of non-monogamous relationships. If you are not a trustworthy individual, there is no way you will find happiness within this Lifestyle. Your partner must trust that you have good intentions and that your actions match your words at all times. This is non-negotiable. If you already have trust issues within your relationship from deceitful, dishonest, and disloyal behavior, you are looking at a long, hard road ahead. Get your house in order. Work on changing yourself and being a better partner. You shouldn't attempt non-monogamy until both of you can find a way to trust one another again.

3. The third thing is honesty. Like trust, you have nothing and are nothing without honesty. Without honesty, how can your partner trust you? Have the guts to be honest about the kind of relationship you really want to have. It doesn't matter how your relationship began, it's about where you want it to go. Sometimes the truth hurts but nothing hurts more than a lie. Give your partner the opportunity to hear your honest thoughts and feelings and ask for the same in return. Be willing to share your deepest desires and show interest in helping your partner fulfill theirs. You may be pleasantly surprised at what you discover.

4. The fourth thing is setting clear boundaries. I can't stress the importance of clear boundaries enough. If you know something will make you uncomfortable, say it. Tell your partner that you're okay with her having sex with other men but you need to be there. Tell your man he can have other partners but you would like to meet them before they had sex. Whatever your boundaries are, just lay them out one by one so that the two of you can figure

out how to move forward. It's okay to feel vulnerable while creating these boundaries. Just understand that at some point your feelings may change as the relationship grows and matures, but how you feel today is how you feel.

5. The fifth thing is you must make and *keep* agreements. Agreements must be flexible and always negotiable. You can't predict every potential problem that may arise, but you can focus on the things you know would be problematic. Always get clarification if an agreement isn't clear. When it comes to agreements, you should learn to implement the 4A's: acknowledge, accept, apologize and amend. Each of us knows what it feels like when a partner breaks an agreement or promise. Oftentimes, we get emotional and act out before taking a moment to understand why the agreement was broken in the first place. In non-monogamous relationships, it is very important to figure this out. Whenever an agreement is broken, it is important to:

a. **Acknowledge** the other's hurt feelings. Listen to what your partner has to say and let your feelings be heard. Make time and space for this to occur.

b. **Accept** that you may view things in different ways. Focus on the commonalities; the differences may not be as important as you think.

c. **Apologize** when needed. If you didn't keep your end of the agreement, an apology goes a long way. It says, *"I understand something I did hurt you. That's not what I intended by my actions."*

d. **Amend** any or all agreements if necessary. What you like today may not be what you're into next week or next year. If this creates conflict, negotiate the terms until the two of you are happy with the resolution. The resolution may be to stop including others in your sex life until the two of you feel connected again. Take that time to reconnect and rebuild. Set a date on which you can revisit the issue of opening your relationship up again.

6. The sixth and final thing is get support. You can't do this alone. I can't stress the importance of getting a relationship coach enough, specifically one who specializes in non-monogamous unions. The typical relationship coach may not understand your issues. In fact, they may correlate your issues to you and your partner's choice to practice non-monogamy. Seek a coach or therapist that is open-minded and will not judge you for your choice to open up your relationship. You can also join different poly groups that can be a supportive community as you walk this different path.

Making the decision to open up your relationship and let others into your life will not be an easy one; nor should it be. It should be a decision based on the love and mutual respect you have for your partner and the commitment you've made to foster his/her happiness. Stop expecting to find sheer happiness in just one person. It's okay to desire love and affection from others, but you must share these desires with the person you've chosen to be with. Stop letting fear hinder your happiness. None of us should be afraid to be who we really want to be. There's no shame in tailoring your relationship to be exactly how you imagine it. Plenty of humans; Black, Hispanic, Asian, White, and otherwise have found happiness and more gratifying lives since entering the Lifestyle. The Lifestyle isn't just for a select few. It's for anyone who chooses to be free of the tunnel vision that has blinded us into thinking we aren't emotionally stable enough to manage how we love and who we fuck.

People always ask me how I was able to free myself from the grip of society's chokehold on our lives. The answer is simple; I just did it. I was tired of pretending to be the kind of woman I was "supposed" to be. Deep inside, I was locked in my own world of unfulfilled sexual fantasies, of untapped desires I could only dream of but never speak about, and I waited 20 years to free myself from that cage. That was entirely too long. I've never felt better about myself than I do today. Sexual and emotional freedom is absolutely liberating! Now, I want to help all of you achieve the same. Use this memoir, my coming out story, my journey, my life, to find your own voice and let the people who matter most know exactly who you are. I won't lie, it won't be easy at first. People will whisper about you, point fingers, and call you names; but fuck those people! Find your truth and live it every day. And if there's one promise I can make, the one thing that has held firm since the day I decided to be true to myself, is that the longer you live in your truth, the better off you will be for it. That's on periodt.

References

1. Blow, Adrian J, Hartnett, Kelley. (2005). Infidelity in Committed Relationships II: A substantive review. Journal of Marital and Family Therapy.

2. Anderson, E. (2012). Sexuality, Identity, and Society. The Monogamy Gap: Men, Love, and The Reality of Cheating. Oxford University Press.

3. Ivell R, Balvers M, Rust W, Bathgate R, Einspanier A. (1997). Oxytocin and male reproductive function. Advances in Experimental Medicine and Biology. 424:253-64. doi: https://doi.org/10.1007/978-1-4615-5913-9_47

4. Marvin Gay and Tom Joyner interview. (1983).

   https://youtu.be/tfIjkcCE_lU

5. Amy Adamczyk, Brittany E. Hayes. (2012). Religion and Sexual Behaviors: Understanding the Influence of Islamic Cultures and Religious Affiliation for Explaining Sex Outside of Marriage. American Sociological Review. Volume: 77 Issue: 5, page(s): 723-746.

6. Lehmiller J. J. (2015). A Comparison of Sexual Health History and Practices among Monogamous and Consensually Nonmonogamous Sexual Partners. The journal of sexual medicine. *12*(10), 2022–2028. https://doi.org/10.1111/jsm.12987

7. For Richer or Poorer: The economics of marriage. www.worldfinance.com. Retrieved 2019-12-11.

8. World Population Review. Divorce Rate by State 2022. Retrieved Mar 11, 2022, from https: //worldpopulationreview. com /state-rankings/divorce-rate-by-state.

Visit

www.Sahartaylor.com

Author & Lifestyle Relationship Coach

instagram.com/dopeassunicorn

facebook.com/sahar.taylor

twitter.com/dopeasssunicorn